THE
TIPSY
MARRIAGE
COUNSELOR

Nicki Grace

NICKI GRACE

CONTENTS

To my wonderful husband Kevin. You are the love of my life, and my king on earth.

Prologue

I rolled over his box of gadgets for the third time this week while trying to pull into the garage and avoid hitting the house. This is ridiculous! I've asked him continuously to clean out the garage so that I could park without hitting stuff. Of course, he says he will get to it, and of course, he hasn't.

Let me take a pause because I'm getting irritated. I need to just take a deep breath and be thankful for what really matters.

It was his things I smashed and nothing that belonged to me. I mean hands down I have better stuff. Oh, you don't believe me?! Listen, when we got married the items I brought into the house made it look like it had value, while his stuff made it look like it had been vandalized. All and all, accidentally destroying that crap reminds me that there truly is a silver lining in everything, you just have to find it.

Maybe that makes me an asshole, but I don't care. Instead, I think I'll take my good fortune and relax. It's been a long week and I need a drink!

INTRODUCTION

Marriage. It's the tattoo you got up the courage to get one night while you were drunk. You wake up the next morning happy and relieved that you finally had the guts to do it. You admire it as a work of art and regard it as one of the best decisions you have ever made.

Or... you question yourself as to what the fuck you were thinking. This is a mess! There is no way you can make a life long commitment to having this attached to you!

If you have felt one or both of these ways (depending on the day), then welcome to marriage! I'm Nicki and for all intents and purposes, I'll be your host. Maybe not a great host, but a host nonetheless. If you are wondering about my credentials, they are as follows: I'm married.

Oh, you thought the list would be longer? Nope. I'm just in it, enjoying the ride just like you.

However, if it makes you feel better, people often tell me that my advice is pretty life changing. Still not good enough? Well, I don't know what to tell you. I did my part by showing up, the rest is on you. My advice will benefit you or in the very least, entertain you, so I suggest you stick around. Plus, you have nothing better to do. May as well skip dinner, lock the dog outside, tell your husband you have a headache, put the kids to bed, tuck away your vibrator and spend some time with yours truly.

Quick side note... I hope those of you that are returning clients from the dating session did in fact bring your own wine. Remember, right before I closed the session, I asked you to bring it? Don't act like you forgot, I will not allow you to live vicariously through me! It's more fun to drink with friends, so if you haven't, get a glass already!

Anyway, where was I? Oh yeah, we were still in the introductions. Sorry, I'm forgetful sometimes (and I fully blame my kids for it), but usually I get back on track. Plus, drinking a little wine makes it all better... or worse... at this point it's not important.

Let me say, welcome newcomers and welcome back to the rest of you. I'm sure you newbies must be wondering what's up with the idea of drinking while I counsel. Short answer, I think wine encourages my uninhibited side so that I can unapologetically announce all the things that everyone is too shy, scared, polite or uptight to say. This method works out great for you because you can just kick back and let me use my expertise (or errors) in the marriage field to get you through the rough, fun and confusing times. Sounds good? Great!

Moving right along. Now, that you know who I am and that I love to drink, you may be wondering what will I be discussing concerning marriage. Honestly, I have no major plans because I'm just going to let it flow. Of course, I have a few subjects to address, such as, honoring the commitment, the kids, the in-laws, finances, illnesses, he can't "keep it hard," you can't "keep it wet," random thoughts, etc. but nothing is off limits, so who knows where I will end up. My unique personality makes me that way. I love humor of all kinds and straight talk, so consider this my disclaimer and don't count my delivery against me.

I cannot stress enough for you to use common sense during the entire session. Some things I say may not pertain to you, but it may be beneficial for someone else to hear. Therefore, don't be selfish, sit there and look pretty while you wait for me to address you again.

My whole goal is to get you to understand that marriage (like any other relationship) is not a one size fits all. It calls for much work and a great deal of role playing. You have to be the wife, the friend, the nurse, the listener, the mother (if you have kids, or a baby as a husband) and even the heroine. Some situations will call for you to stand your ground, while other times you will simply need to bite your tongue and shut the fuck up (this one I haven't mastered so well). Point is, you need to know when it's time to be the bad-ass or the one who brings the band-aids.

Let's reminisce for a second. Do you remember the thoughts you had before you said the famous, "I do?" I assume you had all sorts of plans, hopes and opinions about how it would be. Smiling as you envisioned how your day-to-day marital life would play out. Sure, you expected a few hiccups now and again, but for the most part, smooth sailing. Riding shotgun on the Titanic wasn't what you envisioned and although it's not the reality for all, it is for some.

Being part of the marriage group myself, I get it. I'm familiar with the good, the bad and the botox. Did I lose you there? Botox is injecting your marriage with all kinds of fillers to keep it appearing at its best because on its own, it wasn't heading in the most appealing direction. Don't worry if this is your case, there are no judgements here. We all need some marital botox every now and then, but if your marriage contains more fake injections than it does real chemistry, then you may have a problem. And since someone has to give you the harsh truths, it might as well be me. Lying to yourself about what is, when it really isn't, helps no one. But being honest is hard, which is why I suggest you take one step at a time and don't put too much pressure on either of you.

Marriage tends to go up and down and it's journey will be a different experience from one couple to the next. Frankly speaking, it's a complex commitment that will knock you on your ass if you aren't careful. But regardless of your stage in marriage (i.e. newlyweds, been held hostage for years or planning your escape), I can help. Let me assist you in keeping the flame going, finding matches to restart it, or aiming the fire hose to put that sucker out, once and for all. HA HA HA OMG! I am just kidding! I never promote people getting divorced. I know it happens and sometimes it's the best decision, I just don't ever like to push people that way. The best I could do is help you weigh the facts, the final decision is up to you. Keeping a marriage together isn't an easy task, so choosing to end it wouldn't be either.

Speaking of not easy, did you know the game of "chase and catch" doesn't end at dating, it just changes outfits? I know you're bummed because you hoped you could finally let go, grow out your grays, burn your gym membership, get a "stretch pants only" wardrobe and that poor bastard would still be obligated to love you. Just me? OK... that was awkward.

Moving on, my point is, you can't just stop everything. We still have to be creative, fun and enticing in marriage. The need to learn about and impress your spouse is still just as important (if not more) as it was during dating. So, let's learn and love together. Because whether you adore your commitment or plan to commit the one you adore, we will get through it together and be better for it.

Oh, I almost forgot. Before we jump into the main event, let me share a few secrets about me with you. I love sex jokes, Wednesday Addams is my hero, sarcasm is my safe place and most importantly, I WILL be drinking throughout every session. Hell, I'm drinking right now! That way, you never have to speculate or think I'm side-eyeing you for how many glasses you knock back. Besides, I'll be too busy trying not to tip the scale from tipsy to drunk. I assume highly intoxicated would be unprofessional, right? I thought so. Therefore, I'll stay away from it... but no promises.

However, I will try to stay sober enough to remember this wonderful marital journey that I'm on and I suggest you do the same. After all, 50 years from now, you and I are going to smile and realize we made it... even if the relationship ended 49 years ago.

Therefore, without further ado, it's time for a toast. The night is young and the glasses won't fill themselves. So grab your wine, water, NyQuil, soda, absinthe or whatever you're into, and take a sip. Cheers!

Here's a random thought…
Why is it that when you swipe your card, companies take the money immediately, but once you need it refunded, there are protocols and red tape to clear up before the money goes back to your account?

WELCOME TO GOODBYE

No, not goodbye to your freedom, sanity, clubbing days, or doing whatever you want whenever you want... well actually, maybe it is goodbye to those things... but that's not what I'm talking about. It's time to say goodbye to your preconceived notions about marriage.

Up until you did the do, you were the outsider looking in. You watched other marriages and used it as a starting point to build your hypothetical world of perfection. You weighed the pros and cons and decided it was finally time to take that leap. After all, you said to yourself, how hard could it be? Luckily you were right, but sadly you were also wrong. Marriage can be quite tricky and even if the insight you got while on the outside was correct in some parts, you eventually found it wasn't the whole picture.

Some days (weeks or years) it's magnificent, while others, it's not. There are a lot of components (such as personalities, financial situations, personal goals and state of health) that work together to make your marriage the work of art it is. Even those of you that have been married before are still newbies in a way. The person you were married to before falls under their own category, which basically means, all bets are off. Nothing you have seen or experienced can guarantee you anything. Each marriage stands on it's own.

I suspect that in the beginning, things actually were just like you imagined/hoped. Blissful, romantic and surely the best decision you'd ever made. He helps out around the house, listens to what you have to say, disagreements are cleared up with just a simple apology and date nights are a common occurrence. Let me be the first to say, you got (or had) it good. Who wouldn't want to be married? The love is strong, time together is something you look forward to and the physical attraction is still at an all time high. You could live like this forever.

Then, one night after fabulous love making, he releases a fart that smells so repulsive, you start to question his intent to keep you around. So sorry sweetie, shit just got real and the veil of perfection disappeared or almost certainly hauled ass after an odor like that.

Ok well, maybe that wasn't your exact escort into the "not so beautiful" parts of marriage, but it doesn't matter, I'm sure you get it. Perhaps instead, you had your first real argument, or you just truly realized how messy he is. Regardless of the route, the results are the same, the relationship has now shifted. The abrupt departure of perfect illusions have left you to experience marriage with no sugar-coating, just like the rest of us. Ever so slowly the honeymoon fades and you start to realize it's not always pretty or easy. Trying to convince someone to go right when they want to go left is a headache. Looking at the same face everyday can lose its appeal and feeling like you're taken for granted or being ignored can hurt. You didn't quite expect this and now that you are really settling into marriage, you don't know if you like it.

You find yourself wondering sometimes, what happened to the beginning? It harbored so much excitement and high expectations. You envisioned for years the perfect person that you will end up with. Now that you get to wake up every morning to the winner of your love, you just want to go back to sleep. You wonder… "Am I truly happy? Is my relationship no longer good? Was this a bad decision? Can I change my mind before the ink dries on the marriage certificate? If it already dried, will using some white out suffice?"

None of these thoughts are wrong or bad. It's actually a good thing because now is the time to see what you are made of and how you deal with real life commitment.

Of course things changed, what do you expect? Work is a challenge, family issues occur, the kids become the priority, there isn't enough hours in the day, one or both of you put on weight, you don't have time for date nights, you don't even know what a date is anymore. Was that quick run to the store with him a date? Who knows and you are likely too tired to care. Getting stuck in a routine of "nothing much new" has started to make you feel like a zombie. Even still, I assure you, this is all normal and acceptable, so cut yourself some slack.

When things are easy, anyone can stick around and smile. When they are hard, confusing or boring, people tend to panic or want to end the arrangement. You must remember to remain calm because every relationship has it's problems. Don't go blaming yourself (unless it is your fault) because just like there are rainy days, the sunny ones are soon to come.

Instead of freaking out, assess the situation. Is the root of the problem coming from him, you or both? So what if the six pack he used to strut is now only presented to you in the form of an alcoholic beverage? That doesn't mean all hope is lost, things just get hard sometimes. Or soft and round, in this instance. Trust me, it does not have to remain that way. You are allowed to shift the gears and get that train back on track.

I'm simply stressing for you to wake up! This is YOUR marriage. If you don't like the way it is going, do something about it. If you don't like the cards you have been dealt, reshuffle the deck and if life throws a punch, duck so it can hit someone else. That last one was possibly an asshole move, but desperate times and all. That person with the swollen eye will just have to understand, it wasn't personal, just part of your process.

To improve things have you tried to sit down and talk about it? Are both of you willing to work on the issue? Is one willing to work harder at first to set the tone for the other? Can you keep outsiders opinions out of it? Are outsiders the reason for the problem in the first place? If necessary, do either of you mind cutting some people loose? Are your expectations realistic? Are you comparing your relationship to someone else's? Do you really listen to and regard what the other has to say?

All starter questions that you really need to ponder. Don't rush the answer or put too much pressure on fixing everything right away. If things are really that bad, going to a counselor you can talk face-to-face with may be a good idea. If you need more than talking, then I suggest going paint balling together. That way when he says something dumb, you can just shoot him. Even though the idea sounds like a joke, it might be good to shake things up and let out some long pent up aggression. Then after it's all said and done, not only will you feel better, you won't have to worry about jail time.

No matter what, enjoy the growing process and really take in what you are learning. If you run into it again later on in your marriage (and chances are you will), you should be able to solve it much easier and it won't seem like such a mountain.

Just remember, this too, you can do. Withstanding the storm while it appears everyone else is on the beach is tough but also rewarding once you get through it. Don't try to keep up with the Jones' or talk down about the Davidsons', it will only set you up for failure and heartache. Every couple is in their own lane and should focus on what works and doesn't for their course. Try to spend most of your time meditating on the good and not the bad. Travel back in time and replay the reasons you guys wanted each other in the first place. Was it the way he approached you? Were you drawn in by his smile? The way he took care of you? Did he make you laugh when no one else could? Was it simply because he was a pussy eating champ? All of the above? Whatever the reason, he stood out to you, and in the end you found yourself in love with him. It doesn't matter if your marriage is in trouble or not, it's always a good idea to be reminded of those initial butterflies you had.

After you recall why you married him, ask him to tell you why he wanted you. He may share something you never knew he noticed about you in the beginning. As a result, you will find yourself feeling beautiful and special all over again.

Even if you were each others second choice cause the first one fell through, it doesn't matter. You are together now, so you may as well make the best of it. There is something good about everyone, even if it's not easily visible. New issues arise throughout marriage, but so do new excitements. There is much to look forward to and most of it, isn't bad.

As you grow together you get to know each other on a level that's almost scary. You can finish each others sentences and converse without saying a word. Some people can do this early on in their relationship, but this cool trick of sharing thoughts in a crowded room only gets stronger and more amazing. You get to watch life together and have constant support for when you need it most. People working together is a big part of what makes the world go round and marriage plays by this same rule.

Here's something that's thought provoking. Have you ever paid attention to the fact that a roller coaster is made up of many carts, not just one? This is because no one wants to ride a coaster alone. Part of the fun is the fact that you are experiencing it with others. Watching their reactions and being present to ease their fears and yours, makes it better for everyone. Remember this when you start to feel like the marriage ride isn't all you thought it would be. It's an experience of loops, twist and turns and varying speeds that is best enjoyed with someone else.

Rest in the fact that everyone goes through ups and downs, no matter what you think, life doesn't play favorites. Trust me, you are not the only couple that gets attacked. We are all subject to abuse from the universe from time to time. How you handle it and how your relationship matures from it is the most important thing. Just make sure that when you get through your area of adjustment, you celebrate and be proud of yourselves. Inventing reasons to do something fun never gets old.

People are too trained to think inside of the box, so they don't realize they are limiting themselves. I'm suggesting that you do things different, like argue naked or stare at each other until someone blinks. Then the loser has to do the dishes and the winner gets a strip tease, with tips! Go on a couples retreat, skydiving, or build something together. This is *your* marriage, it can be as grounded or as odd as you want it to be. Continue to always rejoice in your success and find ways to improve from your failures. This is a real marriage you know, so say goodbye to the hypothetical dreams of what could be and welcome to the beautiful reality, of what is.

Here's a random thought…
Do banks have any money on their own, or does it all come from customers/investors?

T HE LAW ON IN-LAWS

The title of this chapter always make me think about people framing their less favorable in-laws so that they can get them arrested. Unfortunately, this chapter is not about that. But hey, maybe I will consider writing a "How to Frame the Family" book at a later date. For now, all I can do is suggest you learn how to make smart remarks under your breath, set the thermostat a little too warm/cold so that they remain uncomfortable or uncover recipes for baking laxatives into their meal. Quick warning, the laxative idea could carry jail time with it, so let's scratch that one…for now.

◆ ◆ ◆

As with any marriage, some in-laws are amazingly breathtaking, and just the sight of them gives you life. Others are utterly bipolar, draining the life out of you. It would be easier if you could just keep the good ones and dump the bad ones, but that's not how it works. When you are married, in some twisted view of reality you have married them too. Just because you hate them and the spouse loves them (or vice versa) makes them no less family. You still have to speak to them, respect them and allow them to be part of your lives. Finding the balance can be challenging and sometimes argumentative because you and your spouse may not see eye-to-eye on the matter. One of you may feel like handling things one way, while the other may totally disagree. How do you decide who's right?

Well, the good news is that it's a choice only the two of you have to decide, the bad news is that still, it may not make the decisions on family any easier. First and foremost, you both need to have a talk about what is and isn't allowed with family. During the dating stages would have probably been the most opportune time to have this conversation, but everyone doesn't get around to it. Plus, I'm sure you were too busy making certain your spouse was sane enough to commit to, so you didn't have much time to think about anyone else. No losses though, you can chat about it now and determine how you two want to handle things. Keep in mind that although mandatory, a conversation about in-laws can be a touchy/delicate topic, so tread carefully. If you have already talked about the functions of family, then this is nothing more than a refresher course for you, but stick around anyway.

What throws most couples off is not talking about the topic deep enough or not sticking to the initial decisions you've made. Both of you must be held accountable for doing their part in the agreement. Pointing fingers won't help anyone's case and holding back won't do the relationship any favors. During this heart to heart all expectations, thoughts and issues should be presented. Here are some questions I'd like you to consider…

How much should the non-related spouse be involved with in-law issues? What are the boundaries for the family? What happens when they get out of line? Which of you two should address it? Can they live with you? Are they allowed to treat your home as their own? Is going into the kitchen and emptying the fridge acceptable? Can they bring people with them when they visit? Their kids? Their pets? Can they stay over anytime they wish? If so, for how long? Are parents treated different than siblings and the rest of the family? Does the non-related spouse have to speak to the ones they don't care for? Will simple small talk suffice? What if you wish to ignore them completely? Are any of them on medication? Have illnesses/disorders that make them difficult to be around? What if one of them gets sick? Is it ok to talk to them about your private matters? Are you allowing them to put stress on your marriage? Is it ok to help them financially? Are they allowed to help you out financially? If so, are they the type to hold their help over your head?

These are great questions to contemplate and open up the airways of discussion. Funny though, I'll admit even with intense conversations and sticking to your boundaries, it can still get out of hand. That's because the law about in-laws is that there aren't any. These people aren't playing by your married rules. They are free to come in and fuck up the balance at any time they want and it's up to you both to correct it.

Sure some of them won't pose you guys any problems, but others won't be so easy. You may find that some of them you simply don't care for and will have to deal with them anyway. He loves his crazy family just like you love your crazy family and unless they have truly crossed the line, you can't just "X" them out completely. Not liking how loud they talk or how much they drink isn't an excuse. If they aren't getting loud with you with an intent to fight or drinking to the point that they are generating problems for your household, then sorry, but you've got to deal with it. This is part of marriage.

I found myself in this very dilemma recently and I'll tell you guys, it's a hard thing to deal with. To make matters worse, it was one of my family members causing the problems and not one of his. As you would expect, I gained more patience and understanding for my relative, but guess what? That doesn't mean my husband did. When faced with a challenge like that, what do you do? On the one hand, I had my husband and on the other, I had my family. Someone that I cared about and was there for me way before I even met him. This circumstance literally gave the saying, "a rock and a hard place" legs to stand on.

Initially, my best advice was to just pray hard and try to be a buffer between him and the in-law in question. Later on, a plan on how to work through it was revealed to me.

Let's start from the beginning. In my conundrum, the in-law causing the disruption was my mom. Sadly, she had gotten sick, very sick and it was only going to get worse. She had been clinically diagnosed with lupus and dementia, but we suspected schizophrenia was also present. I know, right. That's one powerful combo of chaos, pain and sadness.

It made her extremely paranoid, horribly forgetful and ridiculously rude and needy. It was easy to see that as the illness pushed in, her sanity, memory, empathy and logic was being pushed out. You would think we spent a great deal of time being sad and crying over my mom, but hell no. Maybe, this would have been easier if she were just some sick, sweet old lady who needed help from time to time. But no, she was a pure asshole and she knew it. During moments of lucidity, she often laughed about being so offensive towards us and admitted that she knew how horrible she was. I guess this shouldn't have been a surprise because my mom has always been a character. A Bart, Stewie or Cartman character to be exact. I mean, she once used

Miracle-Gro lawn product in her hair because she was convinced if it worked for grass, it would work for hair. Ladies, I was dealing with a whole new version of "Mommy Dearest" here. Honestly, I think she liked to make trouble and then, send you off with a "fuck you" just to mess with your head. She actually called me a bag of shit so many times, I thought she had forgotten my name!

Then, she would calm down, play Mother Teresa, tell me she loves me and offer to buy me lunch, only to tell me to eat shit again the next day. I guess I should be thankful that at least, the illness didn't take her sense of humor.

Other forms of madness she released was calling my sister and I no less, than 30 to 40 times a day collectively, only to ask the same questions back to back and then get offended if she didn't like the answer. If that wasn't bad enough, she would start fights, want to tell me what I could and couldn't do in my house, hallucinate and continually make requests that weren't obtainable.

For instance, she once got upset that I refused to help move her mattress downstairs and load it on a truck to help her avoid pickup fees. In my defense, I was 6 months pregnant and on bed rest at the time, so that was a no go. As you can see, she was psycho and it was tough. I don't think anyone is ever quite ready to deal with that sort of parent, in-law or not. I'm taking a sip just thinking about it.

Her issues were causing all of us issues and high levels of stress. That stress was highjacking our lives and threatening my marriage. She constantly had me on edge, which made me snappy to everyone around me. Imagine the pressure on my poor husband. Getting yelled at by me just because I was in a bad mood, then having my mom under his roof acting all levels of crazy and rude. That had to be a lot for him to withstand, but what could either of us do about it? It's not like we could reason with her or just kick her out of our lives. She wasn't some distant cousin, aunt or uncle I could just write off. She was my mom, she raised me and I loved her. NOTHING, was going to change that. So what did I do? Three things come to mind, right off the top of my head.

First, I did some medical research. I gathered as much information as I could, and sat down with my husband and explained (in great detail) what her illness meant, and how it was and would be affecting her. My goal was to teach him about the illness, but I ended up learning more about it myself. This knowledge helped us both to gain sympathy and lean more on each other during this difficult time. Talk about a silver lining!

Next, I asked my husband to voice any concerns he was having about the things she did. To my surprise, he didn't have as many as I thought he would. I guess the new found sympathy was working pretty good already. The few things that he did tell me about, I tried to fix so that she didn't stress us both out anymore than she needed to. To further clarify, I will give you an example of one of his issues. It was about food. He doesn't like to be wasteful and for some reason, my mom likes to waste everything. She would go in our fridge, request items to eat, then, throw them in the trash after one bite. It's ok with a few things, but she was doing this to the point that it was affecting the grocery bill. As a solution, I stocked my fridge with foods she was willing to eat. Then, when she came over, she ate her own meals and wasn't throwing our food in the trash.

Lastly, I made sure I expressed often to my husband how much I appreciated his patience and help with my mom. There's nothing worse than bending over backwards for someone else's family and not getting so much as a thank you in return. People are happier when they aren't taken for granted and that sort of positive energy is essential during burdensome times.

So there's the three things I did (with the help of my husband of course) to get us back on track. It didn't yield overnight results, and actually took us a few months to get in a good rhythm with everything, but it was worth it. Thankfully, to this day, all of my efforts are still working quite well to ensure that my mom's problems don't ruin my marriage. Also, my mom, is doing fine these days. Don't get me wrong, she still makes us laugh, cry and research tips on how to hide a body, but we'll live.

Making sure that my husband had a voice in this whole ordeal made the biggest impact, in my opinion. His feelings, perspectives and concerns carried weight with me, so I did what I could to ensure he could see that I cared. It was my family after all, so in my mind it was up to me to make the first step in reaching a resolution. We all know that we can't change the family members we are given. If we could, I'm sure some of us would throw the lose cannons back in the pile and demand new ones.

It's a nice idea, but it would never happen. Therefore, you have to make the most out of what you have. Then, when you get married, you have to extend this same understanding and tolerance to the new additions.

I want to be sure that you are not left confused or drawing a blank on this topic, so let's go over some important pointers that you should keep in mind.

Revisit the boundaries you have set for in-laws with each other often, to make sure they are being followed. Try to avoid one on one time with relatives that you don't care for. Ask the other if there is something you can do to make the situation better. Give him the same patience in family matters you would want him to give you. If possible, talk to your spouse before you have a negative reaction to anything his family has done or said. It might go over better if he addresses it instead of you. Stand up for yourself in a polite, but firm way if need be. Don't loan out anything to your in-laws that you can't afford to lose. Don't expect everything to change over night.

I hope that these tips help to keep things calm or diffuse issues all together.

This should go without saying, but although I used the ordeal with my mom as an example, if it is his mom/relative starting trouble, my advice is still the same. Just reverse all my tips and put him in the hot seat.

He should now be the one coming to you to get your opinion on ways to make things easier for you. He should try to be the barrier that blocks his side of the family from wreaking havoc on your emotional/mental state. If he doesn't, then just pull him to the side and tell him how you feel. Chances are, he is so wrapped up in dealing with their issues he didn't think about or notice how much things were affecting you. A simple oversight, but one that you should address. Also, don't forget that although he is the conductor over this because it's his family, you should still be supportive and offer him your patience and kindness as he tries to figure this all out.

As long as you two stick together and consider one another first, it will make your marriage less penetrable from the outside forces that try to break you. If after all of your efforts are exhausted, you find that there really is no way for you to reach a compromise on the in-laws topic, then don't fret. It is highly probable that with all the drinking I do, I may just write that "Framing the Family" book after all.

Here's a random idea...
I can't stand traffic! Why does it exist? Can't everyone just go home when I need to use the road?! It is the worst thing and the presence of it can completely ruin a perfectly good day! I have always heard it is helpful to write a letter to vent out your frustrations when something is really pissing you off. Therefore, I have decided to do something kinda weird and write a letter to traffic and I would like to take a moment and share it with you. Here goes...

Dear Traffic,
You have become a stalker and it scares me. Everyday when I drive home you are in such close proximity that I am truly starting to feel smothered. Everywhere I turn there you are. My fear is that you are trying to detour me from my route home so that you can keep me hostage. I have even moved away from the city where we met and I'm starting to see traces of you near my suburban home. It's becoming harder and harder to escape you.

You act as if I have told you I enjoy your company when I can't stand the sight of you. I am considering having you arrested or filing a restraining order. Every time you show up, words are thrown and tempers flare. Someone needs to put an end to you real soon before I take matters into my own hands.

Signed,

Stay in your lane and get out of mine.

APOLOGIZING

WITH ACTIONS

After telling my husband that I was going to touch his face aggressively if he didn't clean out the garage, I figured apologies were in order. As a loving and humbling gesture, I decided to give him a much needed pedicure. Just like with any pedicure, I rubbed his feet, cut and filed his toenails and made idle chit chat for a calming experience. Afterwards, I gave myself a pat on the back because I did a good job. I even told him "you're welcome" before he had a chance to say "thank you" because sometimes people are too slow to say it and I like to collect my props in advance.

In addition, most women wouldn't dare touch their husband's feet, let alone give him a pedicure. Half of you are cringing at the thought right now and got up to wash your hands to ensure that you didn't vicariously get foot anthrax.

Although, I get how you feel, his feet don't bother me. After all that has happened to me after having kids, touching my husband's feet fresh out of the shower just isn't such a big deal. So yes, I was feeling like the best wife ever and no one could tell me different.

But I should've known no good deed could go unpunished. Instead of giving me endless "thank yous" and "you're the best wife" compliments, he now blames me for his toenails growing back at an angle so sharp, he has to hold his foot sideways in bed to avoid self assault. I truly have no idea how he can be anything less than grateful when I am the one who decided to do something nice for him. Nevertheless, I didn't let his possible injuries rain on my parade. I made an attempt to be nice and when all his socks are shredded, he will smile (or cry) and think of me.

I'm telling you this story because although saying I am sorry is nice and often suitable, other times people want to see actions put to your words. They want you to change up your simple apology and do something that takes effort. It doesn't have to be anything major (unless you really fucked up), just an apology that's more tangible. Put yourself in their shoes. Doesn't saying, "I'm sorry" get old when it's constantly coming from the same person? Over time it loses its weight in sincerity and you may find yourself not wanting to even hear, "sorry" from them ever again.

This is definitely what happens in marriage. Things get old and you have to find ways to make them new. "I'm sorry," starts to sound meaningless, so it's up to you to make it meaningful. Don't get me wrong, saying sorry is good enough sometimes, just not always.

Different mess-ups will call for a certain level of apology. If you forgot to pick up his shirt from the dry cleaners like you said you would, no biggie, you can say sorry and easily pick it up the next day.

Now let's say you threw out his favorite shirt by "accident." Between you and I, I'm pretty sure it wasn't an accident, so maybe you have to do a bit more groveling and let him replace it with another shirt you don't like.

Did you insult his mom? Well now, get the lube because you are going to be sore. This level of screw up requires sex on call and the added bonus of making his favorite meals a couple of times a week. You CANNOT insult his mom! Unless of course, she deserved it. Did she call you out of your name? Slap you? Tell your husband a complete lie about you? If that's the case, then the sex-on-demand and delicious meal coupons are now yours to claim.

The mess-ups will go back and forth and when you are dealing with a lifetime commitment, it's understandable that both of you are going to want something a little more in depth to express regret. On the bright side, even though the role of who's in the dog house will rotate, you guys should always be able to work it out… eventually. That's what marriage is. A loving and intense game of problem solving. You should look at it from the perspective that EVERYTHING can be resolved, even if it takes longer than you would like.

Hold on, let me be clear. I don't want you sitting there thinking "Nicki, are you saying we should just deal with any and every thing?" No my dear, I'm not. There are a few exceptions that may not be best to try and work out. Take a second to notice that I used the word, "may." In my mind, the following things are non-negotiable. To you, they may not even be a reason to flinch. Point is, you set the tone for what is and what isn't too much.

Is someone cheating? A compulsive liar? Do your arguments result in getting in each others faces? Wait. Your arguments don't turn to fights, do they? Fist fights? Really?! Who wins? Yes, I am nosy, but also concerned. All jokes aside, violence is never a good thing and it needs to be dealt with seriously. Fighting is a "hitting below the belt" topic which makes it land above my pay grade. Why, you ask? Because I wouldn't have anything helpful to say. I definitely don't think there is an excuse for it.

If my husband hit me and I tried to stay with him, it still wouldn't work. No judgements on your choices, but my subconscious just wouldn't allow it. From out of nowhere unexplained things would start to happen. Electronics falling into his bath water, ingredients he's allergic to appearing in his food, random loose objects being left on the stairs, his car brakes would probably even fail. I'm just spitballing guesses here, because life for him would just get real puzzling. I can hear the X-Files music now. I'm just saying, I'm not cut out for abusive matters. So talk this one out with someone with a degree who can help you see in a better light because as it pertains to abuse, my lamp is most assuredly broken.

Back to things I can help with. It's not going to be smooth sailing all the time and I know you knew this. You just need to make sure that both of you make each other feel like you care when someone truly messes up. Don't take for granted that the other will always be around or assume they know that you didn't mean to do or say whatever offended them. Show them that it hurts you, that you hurt them. It's so simple to become insensitive when you're married. I think it's the familiarity that does it, but it's still not an excuse. Both of you have feelings and no matter how long you are together, that doesn't change.

For lower to mid-level screw ups, I like to write my guy a letter and leave it for him in his work van or on the kitchen counter. It sets the tone for his work day and reminds him that I actually spent time considering and going over what I did wrong. That I really thought about how it made him feel and deeply considered what I could do to make it better.

He doesn't like to write letters, so on his end, he tends to bring me my favorite cookies or sit me down and tell me all the reasons that he is appreciative for me. Thankfully, we don't screw up often or else there would be no ink left and I'd be as big as a house. Point is, we feel that something quick, yet out of the ordinary are perfect fits for when disagreements aren't too bad. Our basic ways of handling may work for you too, or depending on your personality, you may require a little more or a little less.

For massive mishaps, we kind of surrender the apology action to the offended person. In our relationship, it is best to let the one who has been hurt have full control. Nothing he could think up to do would be good enough so he might as well just let me decide what I would like to make me feel better. I can tell you, it's great to be the one who gets to pick a prize. I don't like it so much when the roles are reversed and I'm trying to make up for what I did or said. Therefore, I try to make sure I'm never wrong and if you remember from my dating session, "Cheating is for Games", I don't like to lose either so I exercise caution.

I don't know why, but for some reason I feel there are some judgmental people sitting around and thinking "You can't just buy your way out of everything" or "some issues have to be solved by talking it out, Nicki." My goodness, you types take all of the fun out of everything! Yes, I know that you can't just buy your way through stuff and I know that there is more to working through your issues than swiping a credit card. But please, get your head out of your ass and keep hanging around. You will see that I come up with many ways and pieces of advice to deal with issues that don't involve gift exchange.

But this section here, right here, is about gifts. Even more so, it's about the fact that when people treat me wrong (spouse or not), I want to see them grovel. I have a deep rooted need to see them come up with ways to make it right. In my mind, sometimes giving materialistic apologies or doing something that requires them to get off their ass is the only way they can mend the bridge that gets them back into my good graces. I'm not the type of person you can continually provide lip service to and everything will be ok. You must show me that you are willing to put in work because I am a structure you would like to remain in your world.

If you are involved with a guy so dense, self centered, weak-minded, careless and rude that nothing he can do/say will make things better, then that's a you and him conversation, not a you and me one. My husband makes me mad and I do the same to him but after some time alone in our separate corners, we talk things out. Not because we *have* to but because we *want* to.

❖ ❖ ❖

Hold on a second, my husband is calling me…

I'm back. The weirdest thing just happened. He asked me if I could get him some cereal. I didn't mind cause I was already in the kitchen. To put it out there, he likes his cereal as an evening snack, with no milk. I eat cereal like a normal person (with milk) so this is foreign to me, but hey, if he likes it, I love it.

Anyway, I bring him his version of cereal (that I'm sure only serial killers eat) in a bowl and he looks at me and says "Wait, where's the spoon?" I look back at him puzzled and say "You need a spoon?" He says "Yeah, how do you eat cereal?" I stared straight at him and said "Ummm, with milk!" and walked away. Talk about strange requests. Yeah, I know I can be a bit of an asshole, but aren't we all sometimes? And if you think you aren't one, you're the worst kind of asshole and I feel bad for you. On second thought, no I don't. That's your problem and one that I'm glad to stay out of.

◆ ◆ ◆

Back to what I was saying. No matter who dropped the ball, we always make it a rule to talk about it, except with this cereal fiasco, of course. That was totally his fault for being weird. My advice is that you WANT to talk things out with each other. It is only the two of you making the rules, so you should be able to reach a conclusion. Being on the same page will go far to prevent a repeat offense. You know what? After the cereal rant, I think it's clear that I'm starting to tilt the scale away from tipsy and more towards drunk so I am going to wrap this up with you guys.

In closing, you can ask him and he can ask you things like... How do you feel? What offended you about what I said? Do you think there was a way I could have said it better? Is that a touchy subject for you? Would you rather I not talk to you about that at all? Why? Or why not? In the future, how would you prefer I address it? Are you willing to let me make it up to you?

There you go, some things to think about. Bottom line, do what you must, buy gifts, apologize, have 12-hour long conversations, screw until your genitals go on strike, I don't care. You have to do what comes natural and keeps the fun flowing. I'm just here to provide insight and guidance and hopefully, enhance my own marriage in the process.

Yet another random thought…
Women have it so bad. We go from wearing diapers when we are babies, pads in our middle years and adult diapers once we're old. Do we ever get a break?! Men don't go through shit!

My Sick Sweetie

I assume that by now you understand my random thoughts. If you don't, let me explain. When I drink my mind is all over the place. I'm lying, my mind is all over the place, regardless.

In any case, yes, I'm counseling on marriage but I do have other thoughts, and seeing that my goal is to help while entertaining you, I share it. It makes things more compelling and I can bet some of my random thoughts you have thought about, too. So much goes on in the world and in my life that I can just spend hours upon hours in my own head thinking about things. The surprising, the confusing, the exciting, the ridiculous, the melancholy…

◆ ◆ ◆

When I was in my mid 20s, I had a job as a customer service representative. One day, one of my regular customers came in. She did her usual hellos and small talk, but she didn't seem like her normal chipper self. When I asked her what was wrong, she broke down crying and confided in me that her husband was in the final stages of dementia. He could no longer remember who she was, didn't speak and spent most of his days sleeping or sitting in his wheel chair with a distant look in his eyes. She was his full-time care taker and admitted that she was worn out from constantly working to take care of him, herself and their household, all while being forced to watch him fade away.

I listened to her with tears stinging my eyes and my heart going out to her. She still loved him, yet she didn't know what to do with all the emotions. Rightfully so, she was sad, angry and confused about all that had occurred and was to come.

I remember telling her that her feelings were valid and that she should never feel ashamed for having them. Against her hopes, desires and pain, this current life was her new normal. She would have to find a way to in the least, hold on to something that gave her a fond and encouraging memory of the man her husband used to be. I asked her was there anything he seemed to enjoy. After thinking about it for a moment, she smiled and said he appears to love watching cartoons. She figured it was because the colors and animation must have reminded him of when he was a kid. Like an eerie version of his childhood self was being projected through him now. I nodded and asked her if she ever watched it with him. She slowly shook her head, possibly confused as to why I asked. Well, I had an idea and hopefully it would work, even if for a short while.

I told her to go home and do ONLY what she needed to do. If it wasn't mandatory, then leave it for another day. The dishes could wait, the laundry could wait, even cooking dinner could wait. Instead, pick up a meal that they both use to enjoy on the way home and grab a bottle of wine for herself. Once she arrived home, I told her that she should setup their dinner and drinks in front of the TV. To add some special touches, I told her to use wine glasses for them both and dim the lights. He doesn't have to be able to drink wine to enjoy his beverage in a nice glass. After everything was all setup she was ready to sit down with her husband and enjoy a date night watching cartoons.

Relaxation of the mind, and being reminded of their blissful quality time was what she needed. In addition, she could pull from her own memory of what she loved about cartoons as a kid to deepen her understanding of why her husband is enjoying it now. Laugh with him at the funny scenes, hold his hand and talk to him like he is right there with you I reminded her, because thank God, he still is.

The next day, I got a phone call at work. It was the lady and she was crying. Happy tears this time, so I was thankful. She told me that she enjoyed herself so much. She couldn't remember ever doing anything like that with him since his dementia had taken over. She even decided that she would start making it a regular thing! She thanked me profusely and said, even if it was only for a couple of hours, she felt like she had her husband back.

I smile when I think of that story. I don't know what eventually happened with them, but I was glad to be able to help.

Sorry to delve into such a gloomy subject, but I am your counselor. We are here to deal with the good, the bad and if necessary, the ever so sad. I truly hope you, nor your spouse have to go through something so agonizing, but life happens. We can't control it and we have to do everything we can to make sure it doesn't completely control us. One or both of you could be battling high blood pressure, cancer, weight issues, postpartum, bipolar depression, diabetes, lupus, etc. and you will still need to keep fighting on the inside, as well as on the outside.

Much too often, dealing with sicknesses makes it so easy to not think optimistically. You get boggled down with the daily to-do and the what-ifs that you can easily forget that there is more to life than just pain. Fortunately, the opinions and inspirations of those around you can be exactly what you need to rise above in areas that you didn't even notice you were sinking in.

I recall when a possible health issue arose with me in the newlywed stage of my marriage. The doctors needed to do a biopsy and it would require that I be put under. I was terrified because I had never been put to sleep before. However, thinking back, I imagine no matter how many times you have done it, it never gets easy. If that wasn't bad enough, after midnight, I wasn't allowed to eat or drink anything until after the procedure was complete. Here it was, almost midnight the day before and the procedure wasn't scheduled until 1pm the following afternoon. 1pm you guys! How the fuck was that going to work? What if I got thirsty or hungry? All I knew was, I was going to be side-eyeing the shit out of some unlucky nurse when it came time to do the famous "count back from 100" drill! Indulging in some of my favorite snacks would have truly helped to calm my nerves and make me feel better, but now they were going to have Ms. Grace the disgrace.

Ever so loudly, I vented my frustrations to my husband. Not thinking he could do anything more than be my sounding board of anger, he surprised me when he said something that made me feel much better. He told me that if I couldn't eat or drink until after the procedure, then neither would he. Somehow having someone suffer with me snack-less and thirsty brightened my mood. Don't judge me! He said that we would get through this together, and just like he predicted... we did.

Eventually, we got the results and everything was fine, my health was still going strong. But the best news was that our relationship was even stronger. It really moved me that he was so supportive and that helped me see him in a whole new light. It wasn't him being poked and prodded, but he was still a part of it. This unexpected situation cemented my belief that health issues are a stress to deal with, no matter which side of the medical madness you are on. You could be the caretaker or the person that needs to be taken care of, it's still hard. You have to watch/experience some of your worst fears playing out. Someone you love is hurting and you can't just flip a switch to fix it.

You lean on each other heavily and everyday it becomes harder to smile or believe you will get through it. Yet, you have to find the strength to do just that.

I will take a moment to remind you that you should keep focus on what is good in your life. If you don't think there is enough good, then create more. Travel, read humorous and exciting stories, visit those that are less fortunate, make fun crafts, write love letters, paint your walls brighter colors, get recipes for yummy but healthy deserts, get massages, use essential oils that relieve stress, get a pet, find new music, or something else just as fulfilling. No matter what you do, don't let the box of sadness close you in. Positive thinking, yields positive results. You guys have each other and that's a blessing. Marriage means you are now part of a team, so walk beside each other as agreed, but don't hesitate to carry one another if there's a need.

Yet another random thought…
So, I was skimming the reviews from my counseling session on dating and they are very good. I'm so excited and thankful that my clients are pleased with my erratic methods. My goal is to help people and make them feel like things can and do get better. Luckily, it looks like I am doing just that! Everyone applauded my random thoughts, my idea to counseling over wine, my comedic approach and they wanted more. Everyone except one person…

Listen up @Littlebopeepliez92, Who the hell died and made you queen? It's called a sense of humor. I don't care if you think I shouldn't drink on the job, this is my fucking company and I do what I want. Guess what, I'm drinking right now. As a matter of fact… I just took a sip for you. I'm sorry that you feel I should have been more conventional and less abrasive in my delivery. Abrasiveness gets results and some people don't like hand holding. Traditional counseling is bullshit, only normal individuals need that. My clients are unique, slightly crazy and a whole lot of freaky (sorry guys, you know it's true). They understand better when it's not presented to them in the same old boring, traditional ways. So thanks for the feedback, but I think it's best if I give your picture to my receptionist to ensure you don't enter into my sessions again.

T ALK ABOUT COMMUNICATION!

Do you remember those fighting or boxing games like Mortal Kombat, UFC or Street Fighter? If not, reference Google please. If so, great! That means you are familiar with the famous K.O. which stands for Knock Out. Now that I have you in the right frame of mind, imagine a match between Talking versus Communication. In this fight it's a tough call and both are close to victory, then all of a sudden, Communication performs a move that Talking simply can't compete with, and it's all over. Communication has won the challenge, beating Talking with a K.O. jab that renders it silent.

I know, me and my metaphors, right. Let me explain. Talking is just words. Communication can also be words, but it's not limited to that. In addition, communication is gestures, body language, reactions and whatever else you can think of to get your point across.

For example, if you are mad and you tell your husband that you are not, all you did was speak. But then, you proceed to slam doors, ignore him calling you from downstairs or intentionally burn his food, then my dear, you are communicating. In a case like this, your words should be ignored, it's all about what you are showing (i.e. communicating).

Communication is so powerful, that at times, it can make talking totally unnecessary. Think about it, animals and babies don't possess the skills to use words, but they can communicate just fine. I know my kid would scream, make gestures or fill up a diaper to get his points across and I understood loud and clear, every time.

Throughout my life, I have seen countless examples on how prominent communication differs from just talking. In many instances, I learned more about people and their motives through what they have communicated and not from all the words spewing out of their mouth. That's why after careful consideration, I came to the conclusion that communication is WAY more fascinating and powerful than talking.

I'll share this excerpt from my dating session that I think provides more depth to what I mean.

◆ ◆ ◆

"I took a friend (we will call her Chelsea) on a blind date with a male friend and myself. With the exception of a nod hello upon arrival, Chelsea's date didn't speak or make eye contact with anyone. She ordered a meal and he ordered nothing. He spent the whole time in silence (with an annoyed looked on his face) while the rest of us talked. It was very obvious to me that he wasn't happy, but I'm not sure if Chelsea noticed or cared. Either way, when the check arrived, it just sat on the table while the three of us continued chatting away. When it came time to leave, my date picked up the check to pay ours. Assuming nothing was wrong (men used to pay the check in my day), Chelsea pushed the check towards Mr. Mute and without a word, he pushed it back. Chelsea looks at Mute and says, "Aren't you going to pay for the meal?" He responds, "I didn't eat anything." Now, at this moment, I'm upset, annoyed, confused and speechless. You mean to tell me this guy knew how to talk the whole time?!! Oh wait, you thought I was bothered by what he said to Chelsea? Nope. I saw the signs, so I already knew the destination wouldn't be pretty."

I love this example. Not just because it is fucking hilarious, but because it is so metaphorically accurate. People (me included, of course) have the random and unfortunate handicap of occasionally missing the strong communication signs in life. If this man wasn't communicating with her the whole time, then I don't know what else you could call it.

I mean, he didn't say anything to her, or anyone else the WHOLE time. He avoided eye contact and he also had his body turned away from her the entire meal. As mentioned in the story, I'm not sure if she was consciously ignoring his signs or legitimately didn't notice, but his thoughts were evident. I know some of you may be wondering what happened next. Did Chelsea respond? If so, what did she say? What did Mute do?

I will end your suspense and let you in on some additional details of the night.

Yes, Chelsea did respond to Mute. She ever so boldly stood up at our table (which was basically in the middle of the restaurant) and made a scene. She said to him, and this is verbatim. "Don't try to pull that shit. You are going to pay for this meal cause I sure as hell won't." She tossed in a few more "Fuck Yous!" and then she walked straight out the door leaving Mute, my date and myself behind. As you would expect, the whole restaurant got quiet, but they went back to eating and minding their own business after she left. My date tried to convince Mute to pay for her meal, but Mute wasn't having it. Her rude, albeit comedic behavior didn't phase him at all. He said he didn't care about her outbursts and that the restaurant could have her arrested for all he cared. So in the end, the bill did get paid and not because Mute stepped up. His refusal to pay meant that my date had to pay for everyone.

Yes, Chelsea did live to date again and no, she doesn't think I'm horrible for laughing at her. She knows my sense of humor, so both her and I have laughed about this story many, many times.

Last, but not least, I have no idea what eventually happened to Mute. That was many years ago, and I assume he has since met his just as silent equal, and is happily married right now. Hopefully, one of my clients isn't the unlucky lady.

So there you have it. A quick (somewhat drastic) view into why you should pay attention to the cues of communication.

I'll admit when I first got married, I never anticipated I would sometimes do more communicating than I did talking. Yet as my marriage got older (forcefully bringing me to age with it) I realized that I didn't always want to talk about things and neither did he. After a long day of work, we just wanted to sit quietly and sometimes not be bothered. This is fine when nothing is wrong, but a problem when things need to be discussed.

It was during one of these moods that I chose to communicate. He said something to me that rubbed me the wrong way. I had already endured a bad day at work and I was extra sensitive and on edge. When he asked me what was wrong, my response was to yell "Nothing genius, I'm just fine!" and walked away. It wasn't really anything he'd done that had me upset and annoyed, but he was sure getting the heat waves of the issue and you know why? Because hurt people, hurt people. Especially in their marriage and some days communicating that hurt is what we do best. Don't get me wrong, it's fine to show him you are pissed if you really are, but if everything is great and you are acting like it isn't, that could mean trouble.

So, am I asking you to communicate less and start talking more? NO, not at all. Communication and talking works hand-in-hand. I'm just making sure you understand that there is a difference between the two, so that you don't unintentionally communicate something you didn't mean. Arguments and crushed feelings often originate from what we communicate to one another, so don't let your relationship suffer any damages due to weak communication skills.

I know you have always heard the saying "the key to a lasting marriage is good communication" and there's a reason for that. Poor communication can destroy things and so many people get it wrong without having realized that they were even messing up! Not to mention, proper communication is one crucial component to the development of your marriage, while a close second is understanding *who* you are communicating with.

What type of man is your husband? How can you tell when he is angry? Irritated? Upset? Calm? Does he get angry quickly? Hold on to little things? Like praise all the time? Shy away from it? Refuses to speak to you when upset? Would rather spend time out with his friends? Likes to talk things out? Gets extremely quiet? Has trouble finding the right words to say? Does he notice when you are mad? Notices, but ignores you? Or is he just genuinely oblivious? Maybe he is the type that doesn't read body language well on people? Or he reads it too well and tries to avoid it?

These questions are child's play compared to the in-depth level of awareness you need to have to understand each other. Oddly enough, the insight could teach you both about habits, flaws and tics that you didn't even know you had. Maybe when mad, you bite your lip or shake your leg. And when happy, you grin and rub your hands together. There could be all these little things you automatically do, and have never noticed them until someone points it out. That's why I'm stressing to you, proper communication, is a must.

Take pride and initiative in mastering one another's behaviors, dislikes, likes, and shortcomings. Do what we do and play a daring and risky game I like to call "You Annoy Me When". It can be fun, but indeed upsetting if you are the sensitive type, or like me, close to your period. However, I think it is good to air the truths and annoyances we have with each other. When I play this with my husband I always demand that he go first. I won't lie, I want to have ammunition to tell him off if I don't like what he says about me. I know that isn't fair, we play this because we love each other and we want our marriage to last. I should be honest and let him do the same, so when we play I behave…mostly.

I know you are dying to know something he said about me, so I will share. He told me that my extreme neatness is sometimes very bothersome. Not able to wait for my turn, I instantly snapped… "it wouldn't be an issue if you cleaned half as much as I did." In response, he just looked at me. Which is his way of telling me to slow down and think about it. So I apologized and let him continue. Honestly, it's not like I didn't know what he was talking about. My extreme neatness is annoying to a few people. It's not lost on me that I am very, very particular with how I like things. For example, once a towel is folded and put away, it irks me if the neater side isn't facing out. Basically, I'm bothered by things that I have learned the average person isn't so picky about. But what could I do? When things aren't in order my brain feels scattered.

As you would expect when it was my turn, I also wanted to address his extreme neatness, or more so the lack thereof. He isn't insanely messy, but he can deal with a lot more mess than I can. He's the type to not drop the clothes in the hamper, but next to it. Or, leave a recently used glass on the counter instead of putting it in the sink because he plans on using it again. You see, in his mind, you don't need to grab a fresh cup twenty minutes later if you get thirsty again, just use the same one. Actually, I'll admit that does make sense on some level, but I just can't handle dirty dishes sitting on the counter. It drives me insane!

So what did we do? We tried (with major emphasis on the try) to do better on both of our ends. He worked to get a better grasp on the way I liked things to look. Putting away towels and household items with me in order to learn my system. For him, I aimed to be more relaxed concerning my approach to cleanliness. Yes I still wanted things a certain way, but as long as he would do some of them to my standards, I would be fine taking care of my other particulars.

As for that damn glass, it still finds its way to my counter, but most days he remembers to place it in the sink. If he needs to use it again he just washes it out each time. Don't worry though, he doesn't need to wash it out as often as you think. We switched to drinking bottled water and that cleared up the dirty glass drama by almost 80%.

Another made up game we play is "What Do You Love About Me?" I'm certain this requires no explanation. It's a game that boosts egos and keeps us in the reminder of why we love each other. We try to make sure we don't repeat the same answers every time we play, so in addition to the physical reasons, we use recent events as answers. Such as he loves that I didn't lose it on the cashier the other day for having a rude attitude, or I love how he starts a load of laundry before the basket even comes near to overflowing... you get the gist.

These are just games we play to broaden our communication, improve ourselves and learn all we can about one another. We feel that if you don't know the little and big things about your mate, it can possibly attribute to you missing some very valuable communication signals in your marriage. What if you guys are growing apart? You know that happens right? Most marriages don't just fall apart in an instant. It's usually a slow progression to their demise. People hold in things and little by little, it adds up. We assume things will be ok and forget that a whole bunch of pennies is what makes a dollar. People don't properly communicate with each other and the relationship starts to fade.

Of course, you don't have to do things exactly the way we did, such as making up games to lighten the communication load. But you should still make sure to check in with each other from time to time. Ask questions such as... are you still happy in this marriage? Do you feel like I am still the husband/wife you expected me to be? Do you find sometimes you would rather be with someone else? Are you bored with our marriage? Do you have any ideas or things you've been wanting to try? Is there anything I can do that I currently don't?

Trust me, it's a good idea to continuously make certain that you are on the same page. As we grow we undoubtedly change. For some, it is subtle, but for others, it's much more candid. No one simply stays the same over their entire lifetime.

However, when you're married, you have to keep that growth happening simultaneously.

So you get it, right? If you want your marriage to soar, you must ensure it's strong enough to fly. By the way, I think people are sometimes slow, so I'll point out that being the KEY to a marriage does not mean communication can SAVE a marriage. You could successfully communicate that you hate each other and that means you have some serious talking to do. Communication is powerful enough that it can strengthen/destroy a marriage, so be aware. It's WHAT is being communicated that determines the course. Therefore, be mindful of what you say, and oddly enough... just as mindful of what you don't.

Oh yeah... another random thought...
What if Google became your enemy and started publicly posting your searches to social media? Can you say... screwed.

P MS GOES POSTAL

My period has the nerve to be two days early. I can't believe this! Why can't the moon make a final decision on which cycle belongs to me? Shouldn't my symptoms be gone now that the actual menstrual is here? Those fucking doctors get everything wrong. What do we even pay them for?! News flash, Mr. MD, it's not just a "pre" to the menstrual, it's a "partaker" during the menstrual. I don't know about you ladies, but these symptoms show up before my period and last throughout the entire yucky, draining process! Every month I'm bloated, irritated, gain new acne residents and realize that people talk way too loud! Ugh!!! I need some ice cream.

*Opens the fridge

Are you fucking kidding me?! Why does he always do this?! He just happens to eat the last bit of ice cream right before I need it. I was saving that just for me! He's so inconsiderate. I don't care that he said he would give me a foot rub and take me shopping this weekend. I'm too bloated to fit into anything anyway and I know he knows it!!! You know what, I'm going to hurt him, just like he hurt me.

Scans the fridge

There it is! His last beer. Well, well, let's just see how you like it.

Chugs the beer down. Grabs a post-it and writes "I DRANK IT ALL" and sticks the note on the empty bottle, then places it on the middle of the counter.

Later that day while watching TV.

He gets on my nerves. Everything about him does. His shoes, how he stands, how he cuddles, how hard his toenails are, how slow his hair grows. He even breaths too loud when he's running. It's called catch your breath quietly!!! Ugh, I can't stand him!!! Why is he even home this early?!

Aww, look at that. It's a puppy. No no no no!!! Don't tell me that puppy doesn't have a home. Poor thing, he's so cute. Look at his eyes. They're so big and sad.

*Tearing up

Why doesn't that puppy have a home? It's sad and lonely out there. I'll adopt you, sweet little puppy. My loving husband and I will take care of you. We have a stable home and you will never have to be sad, hungry or cold, again.
*Full-on tears now and reaches for the phone to call animal adoption.

"Honey, can we get a puppy? We can! You are truly too good to me. I was just sitting here thinking about how much I love you and all the little things about you. Come cuddle with me. I just love you so much. Sure babe, you can ask me anything… What beer bottle?"

*About a week later

Thank God that bloody massacre is over. Tell me, did I sound a bit psycho last week? I'm sure I did and it doesn't bother me at all because I know I'm not alone. Many women feel the same way. I don't know what exactly causes all those issues, but it's crazy. Everything just becomes too much and my emotional state seems to be heightened. All his attempts to be kind seem like some twisted plot against me.

For instance, he brings me breakfast in bed, but I notice he uses the tray with the wobbly leg. He cleans out my car, but leaves the interior light on by mistake. Or the worst thing ever. He brings me McDonald's fries and offers me ketchup with them! Everyone knows you don't eat ketchup on McDonald's fries! The list goes on and on and it's no real reason for me to get upset, I know, but I do anyway and always end up feeling bad. Yet, he takes it all in stride and doesn't say a thing as I scrutinize and judge him with the "you only had one job" eyes.

Now, I'm aware that some women aren't effected by this PMS business. To those women, I say, "Fuck you and also, can I be you when you I grow up?" I mean seriously, feeling extremely sensitive, uncomfortable or having an overwhelming need to be vindictive is no joke. Just be thankful you don't have to go through it. I'll give it to you. You are oh so lucky in this arena, but I'll bet you have something annoying about you. Maybe you are a shopaholic, indecisive, make that face when his less than desirable friend has to stop by, like to move his stuff into places he can't find them, wanted more kids so you tied him to the bed, etc.

My point is, it doesn't really matter what your expertise of lunacy is, I just know you have one or two, or twenty. Everything is not always his fault. Sure, most of the time it is, but not always. We find ourselves getting so agitated at our husbands that we forget that we can sometimes be just as crazy, annoying and frustrating to handle. There will be days that he is going to have to walk on eggshells for you. Mainly because in your fit of rage, you broke all the eggs, but still... he'll have to do it and stay silent and smiling the whole yolk-filled journey.

I think it's good to have friendly reminders that although he makes you mad, you make him mad too. However, if he is a genuinely good man, he won't mind being your punching bag every now and again. Chances are, he probably didn't mean to do that horrible or absent-minded thing he did. So don't cut him, cut him some slack instead, Lord knows we don't need two of you running rampant around the house bleeding out.

You guessed it... more randomness...
I know I've been drinking too much because I am sitting here looking up crazy things men do. Reverse circumcisions and reverse vasectomies for starters. If I were a guy these two things would scare the hell out of me. Doctors are always fucking stuff up when the procedure ISN'T complicated, could you imagine a mess-up on one of these surgeries?

With a reverse vasectomy they are reconnecting penis wires that were disconnected. What if they connect your piss line to your sperm hose? Every time you orgasm you piss all over and inside the girl? And when you need to pee globs of sperm drop in the toilet.

Or for the reverse circumcision, what if the added skin gets stuck or re-sealed some type of way and locks your dick inside itself. Could you imagine a guy at home who needs to pee urgently but has to cut his dick free?

Jeez, so much could go wrong. Men should really drink before they make these decisions, that way they can ponder over all the wacky and scary possibilities like I just did.

READY. SEX. GO

So we grabbed the lube. The hope was to make it easier to slide in. Probably a dumb idea, but we didn't want any friction. This was going to be tricky. I was nervous, excited for him and a bit confused. How was he going to fit that into there? Yeah plenty of couples have done things like this before, but I mean it is the back door! You can't just shove anything in there. Plus, the front door is bigger and more accommodating for this sort of thing if you ask me. Goodness, I was so scared he would tear something. No one had ever used my back door for this before. But I was married and I shouldn't be so scary about every little thing. I needed to trust him and try things for both of our benefits. He took a deep breath, and cautiously applied it. Jeez, it was sticky. Finally, he looked up at me, smiled, then said "you ready?" I nodded and then on the count of three, he pushed. ▓▓▓▓▓▓

WHAT NOW??.
??

wouldn't go in, stupid desk! I told him it was too big to fit in this entrance. But noooo, don't listen to me. He had to have his desk from his college days. He thinks it brings him luck. I just think it brings down my overall decor. I swear, men are just so clueless sometimes.

◆ ◆ ◆

Did you like that intro? I know that you guys were thinking something else. You are so nasty. I'm glad that my mind isn't as dirty as yours. But, since I know you're anxious to get started, let's jump into the real reason most of you even came to my session...

◆ ◆ ◆

Sex. It is a BIG deal. It is one of the main reasons people stick around in a marriage and for others, it is the ONLY reason. When you're dating, the sexual connection and surprises are wonderful. Especially, the first time. Do you remember when you didn't know how much he was packing? Or what he was going to do with that package? You spent your time thinking of ways you could give him the best sex of his life, so that he would fall deeply in love with you, then happily give you unlimited access to his bank accounts?

Awe man, just me again? I must stop sharing with you guys.

Back to the point. In the beginning the sexual activities were fresh and new. Even when you weren't in one another's company, you would spend the day daydreaming about touching each other or new things you could try out. As the kumasutra expert you were, getting bored sexually was the last thing on your mind.

Nowadays, things may have changed. The package you wanted him to pull out so bad, you just wish he would put away. The contents inside no longer excite you the way they used to, so he may as well board it up and prepare it for demolition. HA HA! I am just kidding. I know it's not that bad (I hope), but maybe it could be better. Somewhere between hot and lava-heavy, you guys got cold and iceberg steady. You want to get back to having fun and exciting sex, but it's such hard work. You are too tired and you don't even remember how to do the moves anymore. Sadly, you don't have an endless supply of time to get the grinding in gear, so I suggest figuring out the dilemma and nipping it in the bud.

Did you know that one day a guy's penis won't get hard and your vagina won't get wet? Yup, it's science, but I like to call it genital expiration. Even if it takes until you are both 100, the clock is ticking on the sticking. You'll just be too old to get them to work and they'll be two retired teammates hanging around just to reminisce about the glory days. You'll have to tie his dick to a cucumber and dump a tub of lard into the old vag if you plan on getting those two to love connect. They'll be sending you notes from the grave about regret and how they wish they had more action in life. Do your pals a favor and don't let them down. You're married and sex looks good on any day, on top of anything. If the spice isn't there, add it. If the fire isn't there, ignite it. If the attraction isn't there, slap on some cut out masks of your favorite celebs and go at it. Too much? At least I'm trying. What are you doing?!

Married sex gives you both the opportunity to be each others bitch. Don't want to do that? Well, be each others boss! It really doesn't matter because it's your game to create and play. Reinvent a new normal for what sex should look and feel like in your relationship. The opinions of the world are obsolete because on this turf, you guys are the team captains, lawmakers, cops, judges, jurors, head honchos and referees. It's your collective call that makes it a no, or a go. Having this level of freedom to be physically and mentally naked with each other is nothing short of remarkable. Don't limit yourself by making it boring and plain because that's what you were told or raised to think. You belong to each other, so as long as common respect and love are present, you're good to go.

Maybe you are self-conscious because you have had kids and you think your vagina is in the FUBAR category. Wait, don't tell me you don't know what FUBAR is? It means (Fucked Up Beyond All Recognition). Please keep google within fingertips reach when you are in a session with me. Thanks.

Moving on, maybe your vagina is FUBAR, but who cares, so are a lot of other women's. Therefore, be proud of your destroyed lady dainties. Vaginas are powerful portals. They let kids out and dicks in. How life changing is that? Don't be intimidated by the belief that all men like women so young they haven't been born yet or women so skinny they aren't visible at certain angels. It's just not true.

Some men like women that look like they have lived through something. Those tiger stripes, extra pounds and laugh lines symbolizes life, knowledge, that you can cook and know how to find the humor in things. So embrace it, don't try to erase it. Confidence can go a long way on the scales of desire. Your energy will feed into his and then, you guys can explode together.

I just had a crazy thought. Romance novels and songs are always saying that line about licking you from head to toe. But really, how gross and awkward would that be? I mean, sure you are into it when they are talking about licking your chest, stomach and lady parts, but what happens when they need to lick your eye lid, arm pit, nose or inner ear. Gross! No, thank you.

Anyways, are you finally ready to do the dance and get in his pants? Need some ideas? You knew it was coming, the only reason I'm here is to help you out, of course! Consider some of these tips to enhance or change up the sex game inside your marital cube.

Upgrade your sheet's thread count or at least learn what a sheet thread count is. Nice bedding is a bonus and sex on a cloud is mind blowing. A personal favorite from my doctor is that you do some Kegel exercises. Make that pussy so tight you can toss him from side to side with a simple twist of your hip. Have sex blindfolded. Star in your own porno or re-enact one that you both enjoyed. Bring in some toys, but let him have full control over using them on you. Have a dildo made based off his actual penis. That way if he isn't ready for action, you will have a familiar member of the team that you can get down and on duty with.

Get unpredictable and do it somewhere outside or inside the house that you never have before. Like on the deck or in the garage. Deny him sex, and tease him instead. That way the desire builds and makes the sex that much sweeter. Wear lingerie that he picks out. Buy a wig that makes you look totally different, but insanely hot. One or both of you wear a uniform. Do that showing up at his job thing with just wearing a trench coat, but do it my way. Don't wear some traditional coat, wear a long plastic weather-proof type of raincoat. This way, it doubles as a sort of blanket or mat while having sex and once it's over, the mess can easily be wiped off without leaving any hot-n-spicy stains. Use a timer and make sure that you guys have a sex session (yes that includes foreplay) that is no less than 5 hours long. Is that too much? Ugh, you are such a prude, cut it down to one hour and build from there instead. See how endless the possibilities are? You just have to be willing to go for it.

Now, on to the fabulous sex moves you can try out. All you returning clients heard about these in the dating session, but just for you I have added some new ones.

The Clitosaurus, Ballerina, Reverse Cowgirl, Sword Swallower, The Cat, Slow Dance, Lying Butler, Hot Seat, Camel Style, Spin Cycle, Closed for Business, Iron Chef, Twisted Entry, Spooning Love, Sex Underwater, Butterfly, Scissor Straddle, The Amazon, The Bridge, Open Bar, Riding the Edge.

Did you like those? There are hundreds more out there, you should take a pause from the session and go check some out. I'll wait...

◆ ◆ ◆

Did you find any good ones? I hope so, we all need to find new ways to plumb the pipes. Nothing is better than your man hitting those spots and making it rain. If he doesn't know how to get you there, help him out. Hell, you guys are married now, may as well navigate that tunnel together!

As always, I will offer some words of caution. If you are not a contortionist or you are beyond a certain age, don't play Superwoman. Trying these moves could get something dislocated, relocated and no longer able to be located. I don't want you blaming me or taking a visit to the hospital because you felt bold. Play safe and don't get overwhelmed by how many positions there are to try. Just pace yourself and DON'T RUSH, you are on a marital journey. Save some tricks for the 10th, 40th and 60th anniversary. So what if you're old and carry around a pacemaker, some rushes are worth the risk. Bottom line, shake it up and let loose. Don't be afraid to tell him what you ARE and what you AREN'T into.

Oh, before I exit this topic, I'll throw in this little tidbit. I think sexiness and sex plays hand-in-hand. When someone looks good, smells good and carries themselves well, you find it much easier to want them. You don't know how many times I may be having a disagreement with my husband and I halt the whole thing and say "go get a haircut, then come back and talk to me." I make it clear that looking like a cave man doesn't get anywhere with me. It makes it easier for me to shut you down. But, once he gets all cleaned up, I'll admit, I become that yes girl.

Don't play coy, you know when your guy is looking extremely hot, you are a whole lot more compliant. Having a disagreement with him when he is looking his roughest, versus when he is looking his best may yield different results for him. Both versions of his looks could get him attacked but for totally different reasons. It is a fact that sexiness and good looks get better results, more often. Why is that?

Either way, now that you know, make sure that you make him feel just as driven to be a yes man towards you. Looking like road kill when you are trying to win an argument or possession of his credit card, works best when your sexy is at its full game. You guys will be looking at each other for a long time, keep it sexy, not sad.

However, as a personal request, can you please stay away from doing things that are too crazy? Someone once told me that a girl went down on her guy while he was on the toilet taking a dump. That is the most disgusting, disturbing shit I have ever heard. That girl is going to get splashed with some toxic, muddy water for sure. There's a 100% certainty that I would automatically divorce my husband for a request like that. If he wants me to do that, I clearly don't know him at all and to be frank, I don't want to.

But now that I think about it, if shit's your thing, then you should be in paradise. With all these assholes in the world (pun intended), it shouldn't be too hard for you to get lucky. Now, excuse me while I go sanitize my brain with some wine.

Another random for you… Did that chat just get you hot and bothered? Do you need to find your husband? Simply take a break? Spend some more time on google? Refill your glass?

I totally understand, take all the time you need. I'll be right here when you get back.

P ATIENT PARENT

I'm sure you were thinking "patient," as in a very tolerant person. One who is calm, has patience and is able to endure stress without getting so annoyed, they choke someone. Well, you would be wrong. I meant "patient," as in the medical term. One who has been beat down, subjected to abuse and is in need of medical attention. That's who my husband and I have become and if you are married with kids, I'm going to assume your kid(s) have made a patient out of you, as well.

◆ ◆ ◆

Before I strap you in for this wild, dizzying and joyous ride of where marriage and parenting collide, I would like to take a moment to address those who can't have kids, but really, really want to. It's heartbreaking to feel as if your family will never be complete in the way you envisioned, but I don't want you to ever blame yourself or each other. There are NEVER enough words to comfort a topic like this, but please remember that you still have family in each other and nothing can change that. Find encouragement and meaning in all the great things you do have, as well as what's to come for your beautiful journey together.

◆ ◆ ◆

Now, that I have addressed some of you, let me continue addressing the rest of you...

When my husband and I first had kids, we were naive. Never in all our days could we have imagined that this precious being would turn our world, up side down. Sure, we made plans previous to his arrival. We coordinated schedules, picked all the best lullabies, decorated the room, purchased the highest ranked rockers, froze meals for quick access, baby proofed, blah, blah, blah... but it wasn't enough. This kid had obviously been here before and he WAS NOT playing by the rules. If we looked at him too hard, he'd cry. If we whispered, even on a whole different level of the house, he'd hear. Still, I thought there was hope. Nothing could last always. Eventually, he was going to stop his odd behaviors, non-existent sleep routine, picky eating antics and become normal.

I laugh looking back on it because there is no such thing as a "normal kid." That's like an oxymoron.

Anyway, I wanted my life back or really just some semblance of it. I wanted to be able to hug and play with him when it was convenient for me. Then, go and enjoy time with my husband and various other hobbies. To make it easier, I informed my newborn son of a schedule that I think worked for both of us. In addition to play time, meals, cuddling, rocking, etc. I gave him an additional few hours each week that allowed for miscellaneous things, such as being sick with an ear infection (or whatever illness he chose) excessive diaper changes and even teething. I mean, how fair could I be?! This level of performance I was willing to provide would *surely* deem me mother of the year! But do you think he cared? Respected my schedule at all? Or said, thank you for how generous I was with my time? Nope, he didn't, and even though it annoyed us, we still pressed on. We just knew this new explosive way of life that was taking shape was surely on its last legs and would settle down soon.

It wasn't until he was 16 months old and furiously removing my new, fresh maxi pads from its wrapper and sticking it to the wall that I realized, I was in jail with an unhinged warden that could only be calmed with breast milk and chicken nuggets. He called all the shots and imparted a major shift in our lives that took our freedom with it. This change was, in fact, permanent. Everyday now was unpredictable. Baby warden decided when we went to bed, when we ate, how long our phone calls could last and if we ever got playtime outdoors with the other adults. Yeah, he was running things and there was nothing we could do.

At some point, we assumed feeding him was to blame because the bigger he grew, the bossier he got. So we tried to feed him less nuggets and more vegetables and that didn't go over well. This is the resistance that got us thrown into the torture chamber, where he produced (on demand it seemed) overflowing diapers that oozed up his back and out of the side of his onesies and we were forced to clean it up. Then, as a final blow, he would keep us up all night so that sleep deprivation would make us weak and weary enough to adhere to his demands without complaint.

Bottom line, we were losing. Hell, we had already lost, we just didn't know it yet. The whole situation left us feeling duped. Sort of like how you feel when you get hired for a job with expected assignments and duties, but over time they start to slide in all sorts of things without warning or preparation. No... I take that back, it's not like that because at least with a job you can go to the boss and renegotiate terms and demand respect, with a baby, all sales are final. Even if you think...

◆ ◆ ◆

You know what? You guys are going to have to give me a minute because I'm getting dizzy. I was feeling good from the wine, but now I think I'm going to be sick. I am sitting in my office with the door shut and my toddler is in here with me. He keeps passing gas and laughing about it. He stinks so bad, I keep having to look up to make sure a full grown man in desperate need of a colon cleanse hasn't taken his place. I don't know if he's trying to make me pass out so he can get into the cookie jar or replace me once and for all, but this smell has some terroristic abilities. I mean, MY GOODNESS, what the hell has he been eating? Are these foods the FDA actually cleared? If he keeps this up, I'm going to have to consider trading him in for a less offensive model.

◆ ◆ ◆

It took about thirty minutes of an intensive, uncooperative diaper change, but finally I'm back to fresh air. I passed my gas box off to my husband. Now you, I, and a fresh glass of wine will finish this conversation on the deck. It dawned on me, that being able to pass the kid off to catch a break is a nice little bonus in marriage. Sure things aren't the same as it was before kids, but it's nice to be able to tackle this with someone. By the way, for those of you that have had to parent alone, YOU WIN! You are officially the strongest and bravest people I know and I mean that from the bottom of my heart.

Back to the topic. Like most of you, of course, I sometimes miss the dynamics of when it was just hubs and I. We would come home from work, enjoy a good movie, a quiet dinner, then fall asleep cuddled up in bed. Toss in some spontaneous date nights, fun-filled vacations here and there and that basically summed up our lives. It was beautiful, reliably predictable and calm.

Then, we had kids and so much changed. Our new after work routine was chasing little people around, yelling threats throughout the house, negotiating to avoid or end a tantrum, eating dinner standing up and going to sleep with tiny feet on our face. What a difference! No matter how hard you try, kids just create a life that you can't prepare for. They amp up the pace and volume and don't even apologize for it. But, on the flip side, they are cute, caring and freaking hilarious. They continually say exactly what they are thinking, love you without strings attached, and maintain an energy level higher than you ever thought possible! I mean, seriously, where do they get their training? And where can I sign up? It's like they're part battery pack. I thought they were new here, so in retrospect, should be weaker than us. This just doesn't seem scientifically possible, but somehow it is.

Yet day after day, and no matter their intent to kill us through energy depletion, we still are happy to love and keep them around. They gives us something to look forward to, something to hope for and another reason to be grateful for our parents.

Even still, as wonderful as all that can be, raising them is… at times… very difficult. You have to do so much, but you can't possibly do it all. Which means you must invent ways to balance self, marriage and family needs. Challenge much? How in the world are you supposed to make time when there is no time? Find energy when there is none to spare? Touch each other and not fall asleep midway through due to sleep deprivation? Truthfully, I'm not entirely sure, but I know survival is possible.

Take a deep breath and allow me to point out that you aren't crazy. This juggling act is hard for EVERYONE. Failing to keep up in every arena of your life doesn't mean you are doing a bad job, no one can be a winner all the time. You just have to keep at it and try not be too negative on your worst days. I know, I know, that sounds good for a pep talk, but it still leaves you wondering, what can I do? How do we create this much needed balance between marriage and parental duties? Is it even that important to consciously try? Well, if you want your marriage to stay intact, once kids enter in (or explosively out, if your vagina has anything to say about it), then you definitely have to get creative.

Speaking of explosive vaginal exits, let me veer slightly off topic for a moment. I know some of you may have kids in the marriage that aren't biologically yours. Maybe you adopted them or they're your step kids. However, just because your body was spared from birthing a scene from the movie, Alien, I'm aware that you still have your own unique hoops to jump through. If you are a stepmom, for instance, taking on the role of "not the momma" can be a shit storm. That kid may be bad as hell, but you know what? It doesn't matter. Even if you saw their "Children of The Corn" membership card with your own eyes, you are still obligated to love and make them feel special.

Kids act out and their whole reason for doing so may be because they blame you for their parents not being together. In their mind, if it weren't for you, they would be living happily ever after right now. Give them their space and don't try to jump in full force. I had a stepmom that did that once and all of her possessions (and yes that means clothes, underwear, wigs and tampons) ended up on the front lawn, thanks to yours truly and my big sis. So, I know what I'm talking about and I also know that kids can smell desperation a mile away.

Therefore, slowly… and I do mean slowly, initiate things for you two to do together. Going to see a movie that they will like, or helping them with a school project is a good start. Whether or not they live with you, you can allow them to pick out things to add to the home. Maybe, hang their school drawings on the fridge, let them design their own bedroom, include photos of them around the house or let them choose what will be for dinner on Friday nights, etc.

The goal here is to get them to see that you are not the enemy. As they begin to realize that you care and only want to add to their life, not take away from it, things will get better. Eventually, it will dawn on them that you do not want to take their dad away or replace their mom. They'll see your loving intentions and understand that all their less than desirable behavior, is making them miss out on knowing an awesome person.

From a different perspective, it's common that another family blending setback could be caused by your "I promise to love until the day that I die" husband. Shocking, because he is supposed to be your main "go to" for issues. The one who helps things flow, protects you from the hurt and is there when no one else understands. Even still, bringing you fully into his kids' life may be difficult for him. It may seem that he simply doesn't want your input on how to raise his kid(s) or he may automatically choose their side on everything. That can be devastating because it's hard for a family unit to work if he can't discern that the child has to respect you, as well. It may be *his* kid(s), but it's *your* union that gets affected by this. However, possibly without realizing it, he is allowing them to get away with murder because he feels bad for them and his guilt is throwing off his judgment.

One time this guy told me that the reason he spoiled his kids was because they had lost their mom in a car accident. In his mind, they had experienced more sadness than anyone ever should, so he wanted to make all their days as happy and fun-filled as he could. Although, this behavior could be damaging for kids in the long run, a parent that has enormous guilt can't see the "what happens when" they can only feel what's going on now.

If you are in a situation like this, it's going to be a bit rocky there for a while, but I have faith that you can get things solid. As always, you will need to talk about it. Be sure to use complete honesty when voicing how you feel and be just as unbiased when listening to him. He may be very stubborn on this subject and completely against even talking about it. Every attempt you make to have a deep conversation, he may refuse.

If this is the case, you will have to stay calm, inject yourself with a high dose of patience and approach the matter from another angle. Subtly show him that you are working hard to make everyone in the family feel accepted and special by doing things that force him to see your efforts. For example, buy the child(ren) an "I love you" or "thinking of you" card for no reason and have him sign it after you do. I guarantee he will take notice of what you did. He may even ask you what made you think of giving them the card. Or comment on how sweet your gesture is.

If he asks you questions about your selfless behaviors, use that as a small entrance to get the ball rolling. BUT, respond carefully and nonchalantly. Remember, this is a conversation that he isn't ready to have. Past attempts prove this, so verbally opening this can of worms is something he will have to do. Don't try to dive in deep and unload all the drama you have mentioned to him in the past. Instead, let your your answer be something simple like "I was noticing that (insert kid name here) avoids me a lot. I think that if I reach out to him/her, then they will see that I am really trying, and hopefully meet me half way."

Even if he doesn't take the bait and give you the talk you so desperately want, TRUST ME, he will notice that you did something nice for his kid. Instead of talking to you he may take a different route and start speaking more to his child about being kinder and more respectful towards you.

Until things improve, continue doing random acts like this. In case you are stuck on more ideas, you can also invite the child to do activities in his presence, or plan a day where you and he can go to their school to surprise them for lunch. I hope that you are catching on. You need to force him to deal with it, without forcing him at all.

Eventually, the child will come around (eliminating the need to discuss it with your husband) or your husband will come to the realization that there's nothing to be afraid of and finally broach the subject. Again, it will not happen overnight. Majority of the work in the beginning may be on your shoulders, but do you recall that "for better or worse" part you agreed to? Yeah, you can guess which piece this is.

Stay focused on the destination, so that the flight doesn't get you down in this dilemma. Middle ground must be reached and patience is paramount. No one is going to become the Brady Bunch overnight or maybe ever. But landing your family somewhere between "The Cosbys" and "The Gallaghers" from Shameless will suffice just fine.

It doesn't matter which of you are the stepparent, you must help each other out. He could be starring in his own version of "Are We There Yet?" as he's trying to adjust to your brats. By the way, that was a movie reference for some of you they didn't get it. It is hilarious and those kids are bad as hell, you should check it out. Anyway, once you all are no longer at each other's throats, you can move forward to figuring out how to keep the family unit functioning as it should.

Now, let's get back to the main question. How do we create the much needed balance between marriage and parental duties? It is my belief that the answer to this balance lies in setting boundaries, making schedules and doing our best to stick to them. For example, determine bedtimes, meal times, play times, family time and mom and dad time. If you co-sleep/room share with your kids, decide when you should start the shift of getting your room back. Figure out what disciplinary actions (if any) will be used in your child rearing. Who executes it? One of you? Both of you? Regardless of your choice, remember a united front works best. That means you two need to discuss things first, or risk your kids playing you guys against each other.

Another pointer is to assess their needs from you as a parent and determine how you can most efficiently meet them. Are family meal times a priority? Can you make it to every game they have? Every show they're starring in? Assist them with every assignment that comes due? Maybe you can, or maybe you have more than one kid and a hectic work schedule, so it isn't possible. If that is the case, then be up front with them and explain your dilemma in scheduling. If you can only come to certain activities, let them choose your spouse, a friend or relatives to attend the others. I know it may be hard, but it's better that you talk to them instead of trying to play Superwoman and breaking your word.

One more suggestion for balance is to decide what household tasks they should be responsible for. Even if you have done this in the past, re-evaluate again. Maybe the kid(s) have matured and are ready to handle more responsibility. Within reason, of course, give them assignments that help remove duties from your plate. Doing their own laundry, making their own snacks/meals and cleaning their own room(s) are good starters.

Once again, don't forget about time with one another. You and hubby are the foundation for the family and if you aren't solid, then the whole structure will collapse. If your kids are young, have family/friends babysit so that you can do something out of routine. If there is no one around, splurge on a professional babysitter. The occasional expense for this is nothing compared to what it will do for your sanity and union, so don't think of it as spending unnecessarily.

If you have no family/friends to help and no money to hire someone, don't worry, just be creative. Get your kid set on a schedule so that they are asleep by a certain time. Then once they fall asleep, sit together and have dinner by candlelight, watch a movie, play board games or just talk. The point is, find a way to keep your connection because you *and* your marriage will need to recharge before you re-enter the fun family chaos.

It's a lot to juggle and no matter how brilliant you are, some days one of your roles will have to go a little slack while you catch up with the others. Occasionally accepting defeat can sometimes be the answer, while other days you can buck back at life and win.

Deciding to bring kids into your marriage is the most fun, unpredictable, stressful, blissful, terrorizing and loving experience you will possibly ever have. Try not to over think things that you have no control over. Your life with your family is a blessing and worth all the ups and downs you go through. Remember that when things get cloudy.

Now, to those of you that don't have kids. Perhaps you want them, just not right now or maybe you don't want them at all. Playing the fun aunt or being mommy to an adorable puppy could be more your style. Whatever your reason, I am jealous and at the same time feel sad for you.

I am jealous because, HELLO… FREEDOM! You get to do what you want, when you want. No need to worry about diapers, tantrums, mommy brain, endless laundry, additional bills, lack of sleep or having to punch out other kids to defend yours. It is definitely less hectic. Things are truly easier when you are just dealing with two in your household and not three, five or twelve. Can you believe it, some people have ten kids? How are they still standing?! Either way, I totally get it.

Yet, on the other hand, I feel sad for you. Although, I agree that you know what's best for you, I just can't help but think about my pre-kids self. When I first got married, I actually didn't want kids. I felt that whole baby thing wasn't me and I would prefer to not have the extra complications.

Now that I have my dear hearts I see things differently. You may be thinking "well you have to, duh, they are here now." But no, that's not it. It wasn't about them as much as it was about me. It made me more patient, kind and I saw the world in a different way. Yeah, it is scarier when you have kids, but also more beautiful. It's them that will keep the world going and it's a piece of you that will continue to live on. I can't speak for every parent, but I smile when I realize that in raising them, I am planting and preparing a part of myself in hopes of making the future, better than the present.

All the additional, "I love yous", watching them grow up and feeling like there is something more important than yourself is just a bonus.

Sorry, I'm not trying to get deep with you because, like I said, I respect everyone's decision. Truth is, you may be a horrible parent. Your suspicions could be spot on and you just spared a child from a very unbalanced childhood with you. So for that, I thank you. Plus, it means you are free to babysit mine. Talk about a win, win.

To the rest of you that are planning to have kids and it just hasn't happened yet, I say... see you suckers in the parent trap. Man, it will be fun to see someone else tortured by their kid(s). HA HA! Sorry, not sorry.

In closing of this topic, you parents out there stay focused and roll with the punches. Yes, kids keep us on our toes, but those little angels can also bring you and your guy closer together. Think about it, you both are working as a unit to shape a life. A portion of this child's successes/failures will be linked back to you and what you instilled in them. That is an *extreme* bonding experience. It gives you more reasons to trust, listen to and embrace the strengths/weaknesses you both offer. You get to see one another from a different perspective and gain new respects and admirations along the way.

Everything will be fine, being a parent won't kill you, it's just undoubtedly going to kick your ass. That's ok, you can look forward to the down time you spend together in the hospital while your battle scars heal.

Another random thought for you…
I wonder how long it will take me to get into the shape of a supermodel when I go on my new diet. Getting to my goal weight should be easy because I can give up all that bad food without a fuss. Well, of course, I would still need to have my daily glass of wine. But, that's fine because doing my workouts should burn those calories. Oh yeah, I can't forget, I also must have my weekly pack of mini donuts. If I don't have my sweets, someone's getting cut.

Oh no! I almost forget my weekly order of french fries. Let's see, wine, donuts, and french fries, that's it. Wait, I have to have my weekend breakfast with eggs, bacon, grits, biscuits and orange juice. That truly is the only real way to start the weekend. So wine, donuts, french fries, eggs, bacon, biscuits, grits and orange juice. This all sounds so good. What we were talking about? From the looks of it, I was making a grocery list. Sounds good to me. Let me just add ice cream, frozen pizza, hamburgers and hotdogs and the list is complete. Off to the store I go… I'm hungry.

I DO... BUT NOT REALLY

Listen closely, I am a bit drunk right now, but I decided why not keep counseling. These clients came here for some truth and a show, may as well give it to them. And if a show is not what you want, sorry... you just got front row tickets anyway...

◆ ◆ ◆

Ever just wanted to tell somebody fuck you, your opinions, your emotions, the horse you rode in on, where you came from, where you're going, the life you live, your next breath and your very existence? If not, keep living. If you have, I like you better. Originally, I only reserved this level of distaste for student loans, but as my life progressed I decided that there was room for one more.

The newcomer to this level of loathing is two-faced people. You know who I'm talking about, flat out liars, the "need to be liked by everyone" ass kissers, fakers, extreme opportunists, yes, those people! Ugh, they just get under my skin! They endlessly pretend to be one person amongst one crowd and then, another when in the company of a different crowd. It's like, pick a side you Indecisive. Chameleon. Fucker. Do you have low self-esteem? Did you not get enough hugs? What the fuck is wrong with you?

Hmmmmm, could I have a bit of my mother in me after all? Whatever, who cares!

I just don't get it. If you don't like someone, be clear about it and don't pretend otherwise. It's not hard to decide how you feel, it's just the weak little rat in you that won't let you stand your ground for a change. Either you're hot or cold, love them or hate them, want to kill them or cure them, it isn't hard!

Now understand, I'm not saying that you can't have mixed feelings about someone or that you can't be the type of person that changes the way you act depending on who you are around. That's called blending in, being polite, working well with others and that is understandable, respectful and in some cases, takes major discipline. However, that's not what I'm talking about.

People like this don't have mixed feelings, they are simply two-faced assholes that don't care who they hurt or what they destroy. They are detestable to me and such a mystery at the same time. How can people be so relentlessly for themselves? How can you genuinely not care who suffers as longs as it isn't you? It seems inhuman to me in a way, to be so intentionally cold. Yes my dears, there are people like this, and we encounter them everyday.

Sorry for the rant. I know none of my wonderful clients are like that. You guys wouldn't hurt a fly. However, I had no idea these types of people annoyed me so much. Better go take a nap and talk to someone about that.

*The next day

Hey guys, I'm back and no longer drunk. Sorry about yesterday, sometimes I just have a need to unload the angry cart, you know? Either way, I'm a whole lot calmer and I'm ready to get back to the topic.

To clarify, I'm still infuriated that people can behave in such a "it's all about me" manner, but I want to make sure that I give you the levelheaded insight you deserve. Therefore, in order to explain myself better, I will start again.

I knew this lady years ago that was sweet, kind, clueless and a hopeless romantic. She had been seriously dating this guy for a few years. To clarify, by serious, I mean that she thought there were wedding bells in their future, but he couldn't keep it in his pants. Anyway, she had a kid by him and she adored and loved him way more than he earned.

Several times he had been caught by her and various other people cheating. He had even made kids with other women that she chose to accept and treat like her own. Like you would expect, every time he was caught he would beg her to stay with him. He told her he loved her and that he would do better and of course, she believed him. But, you know the truth, he wasn't a good man. He was a user and a neglectful boyfriend and father. Of course, people often told her to leave him, but she wouldn't. She loved him more than sanity and dealt with the pain because she felt positive that one day he would give her his all and be the family man that she hoped he could be.

The brutal push she needed to move on finally arrived in the form of an STD, when she tested positive for HIV. How horrible is that? She gave him unconditional love and in return he gave her a death sentence. To make matters worse, she found out that he knew about his diagnosis all along, but didn't think he should tell her because he "assumed" she wouldn't catch it.

It was a depressingly pointless situation that didn't need to happen, to say the least. Sure, she could have walked away one of the many times he cheated, but she didn't. Nevertheless, the worst she could be accused of is being stupid, naive or even hopeless. But he, was relentlessly cruel. Why wouldn't he just let her go? He didn't have to keep lying. He didn't have to put her life (and countless other women's lives) in danger. If he truly loved her, he could have even confessed and then left her until he could get his head (the big and small one) in order. But, no way! He couldn't do that, he had to have it all. Women wanted him, so of course, he had to sleep with ALL of them. The lies didn't matter to him, it was their problem. He actively played on her emotions and infected her, when all he had to do was stop. That, my dears, is the type of fake person I'm talking about.

They cause unnecessary problems, pain, resentment and stress to others. They live to take and take until they have drained the source only to move right along to another. Understandably, every encounter with one of these types isn't always as detrimental as the example I gave, it's just the same concept over and over. A person living a double life, using various forms of manipulation to get their way.

It's bad enough to deal with a person like this at your job, at an annual family reunion or occasionally at a mutual friend's gatherings, but it's a whole different level to be married to someone like this. I hope that none of you are ill-fated enough to be married to a person of this caliber, but many people are tied to corrupted individuals like this and they don't even know it. Usually things go something like this...

The unaware spouse is believing that all is well. Sure, they may have gained weight, become less adventurous or just gotten so boggled down in taking care of the household and others that they didn't realize that their spouse could no longer be trusted. All along, the chaos creator is cheating, lying, or even plotting to leave them holding the bag. For some reason, the deceitful one feels they are entitled to do what they want. They put forth no effort to repair the relationship or uphold responsibilities, but to them their spouse is to blame. They cause all the issues, but act like they're the victim. Instead of airing their dirty laundry and being upfront with you, they smile and pretend all is well. Get them in front of friends, co-workers or family members and they say it's you who is killing the relationship.

This is simply not right. I'm not sure if they do this because they want sympathy or want to lessen their increasing guilt, but it's pathetic.

Let me slow down. I am not saying that you can't vent to others when you are frustrated about your significant other. It can be a very good idea to talk things out or get advice from a level headed and trustworthy source about your problems. What I am saying is you can't keep your relationship from ashes while also being the arsonist. You must pick a side (the right side) and stick to it. Roll up your sleeves and stand firm in the vows that you've made. You have a job to keep things great and make repairs when needed. This is your investment owned by your heart and soul. Some respect is due to it. Everyone veers off course sometimes, does things that they shouldn't or forget the whole reason they fell in love in the first place. That doesn't make you horrible or fake.

However, it's when you realize that things are off track and instead of fixing them, you start placing blame and not owning up to your part, that it becomes distasteful and wrong. It's common to not want to accept responsibility or admit fault, but do it anyway. It's not just because of your marriage that you do the right thing, it's because of your character. You should always aim for the high road regardless of the situation, because life is less about what happens, and more about how you handle it.

In order to keep your marriage strong you must pray together and have faith. I understand that some of you are not into praying or believing in such things. Nonetheless, there are many couples that do and I am one of them. So excuse me for a sec while I address them.

God is powerful, awesome, wonderful, all knowing and never wrong. You can trust that he will guide you to where you should be and what you should do. If you find yourself facing problems in your marriage and don't know how to get back on track, talk to the Most High God. I suggest doing it alone first and then, praying together with your spouse, second. Or the other way around if you think that works best. If your spouse won't pray with you, that's fine. God doesn't require two, in order to hear one. He will still listen, direct and protect. Just continue to stay humble and positive.

He WILL answer... when the time is right. Pay attention to the signs and keep communicating and loving each other while you wait to receive guidance. Faith can move mountains and God's desire is for you to win.

Back to everyone, again. I hope that marital issues aren't rising or overflowing in your relationship. That neither you or your spouse are doing underhanded things to each other to weaken your commitment and set it in motion for disintegration.

Has anything I have said made you realize that you or your spouse are possibly, doing just that? Initiating (or contributing to) the negative strain on your marriage all along and didn't even know it? It's your lucky day because I have some deciphering questions to help you out.

Are you constantly hiding things? Maybe, you are just flat out lying? What would your reaction be if you found out they were doing this to you? Are you harboring some resentment towards them? Have you started planning a life without them? Have you cheated? Plan on cheating? Are currently cheating? Do you think you would be happier without them? Do you bad-mouth your spouse behind their back? Are the things you say, things you haven't told them? Do you paint them in a bad light to others?

I think these questions help even if nothing is wrong. Answering them contributes to you staying grounded or revealing something that you didn't know was there. You know what? I would like to elaborate on the last question about painting someone in dim lighting, by providing you with a funny example.

I have a male cousin who is a professional masseur. He takes pride in his job, has male and female clientele alike and wants to one day open his own massage spa. His dad, a man who measures if a guy is a "real man" by the work they can do with their hands, frowns down on my cousin for this. Since he is a farmer and was raised in the country where you "ate what you killed," he can not fathom why a man would want to work in a profession like this. One day, my uncle was asked by someone what my cousin does for a living, he replied, "He rubs oil on men for money."

Now, hands down that was a witty response, but come on! Yes, he uses oil and he has clients that are male, but the oil is a tool for his work, and what about the female clients?! He made him sound like some type of prostitute! He didn't just paint my cousin in a bad light, he burned the paint brush and went at it with crayons in the dark! Please don't do things like this to each other. Omitting truths can be just as destructive. Making each other look weak, selfish, victimized, rude or anything less than what they really are for purposes of destroying their image in front of others is not right. Have some class and don't be an ass.

Before I completely leave this example, something just dawned on me. It's possible that I would've considered hiring a male escort. NO, NOT NOW! My husband has got me satisfied in that department, but when I was younger and dumber… say like in my very late teens to early twenties. During that time, I was convinced that most guys didn't know shit about pleasing a woman so I could see myself trying interesting things. Of course, upon initially thinking about it, the idea was disgusting because when I think of escorts, prostitutes, hookers or whatever you want to call them, I think of people that are licking, sucking and fucking whoever can pay to play. But one day I was watching this movie and this guy ended up becoming a male escort. He was highly attractive and would do basically whatever the lady needed him to, and that got me to thinking. Switch the guy, toss in a few additional tweaks and the younger, wilder version of myself would be placing my escort order routinely. Let's say for instance, times were ridiculously hard and ALL of your favorite male celebrities started sleeping with their fans for an affordable price. Hmmm, maybe around 50 bucks. Cheap, I know, but it's hypothetical and like I said, hard times. Anyway, I could think of a few (ok, 50 plus) celebs I would've surely hired. Short of making sure they provided me with clean STD results and wrapped up the stick in a couple of condoms, they could count on me for supporting the cause. You can look at me sideways if you want. I know some of you would have been right there with me. The rest of you are checking your wallets as I speak, wondering if you could get set up on a flat rate for services. Then again, maybe I've just had too much to drink…guess we will never know… back to the topic.

Once you have both decided that you are in it for keeps (something that should have happened at "I Do"), then, stay planted. Don't let life, people or circumstances move you. Tough times are no excuse to play both sides of the tennis net with your marriage. Neglecting what you have just because you think the grass is greener on the other side may just get you stuck in the fence. Even the most beautiful flower had to endure some shit (farmers call it manure) to grow. Just plow through it and you'll be fine.

Even if it's not something you wish to work at anymore, that's fine too, just be sincere. This major decision is going to affect their life also, it's only fair to let them in on it. Tell your spouse that you don't think things can be saved, that you want out or (if it's the case) that you want someone else. Maybe you grew apart, one of you was horrible to the other or both of you were horrible to each other. Regardless, it was decided that ending it was the best move for both of you. No one is immune to breakups, but sometimes calling it quits is the more mature move. If your plans are to leave or quit trying, you should make that crystal clear. Causing someone devastation by your actions or escape plans will surely get karma looking in your direction.

Phew, I've said my piece and I feel better, don't you? I think marriage gets a bad rep, because we don't always want to put in the work for it. We forget that a union like this requires high levels of give and take. Emphasis on the "give." Remind yourself that making your marriage last takes conscious effort and never forget the most important question of all, do you really want your marriage to last? When I asked-myself this question, the answer was 100%, both feet in. YES, I do! Now, I pass the microphone to you and ask... but do you?

Another random realization....
Was I supposed to be trying to start a diet? Back when I made a grocery list? I do that every single time I am supposed to seriously start a diet! Guess we all have some things to work on.

PAMPERING POINTERS

When I think of the word pamper, I always think of spas. I have no idea why. It may just be because I love spas so much or because every time a spa is advertised the word, pamper, is sure to follow close behind. Whatever the reason, I know one thing for sure, pampering is important. The need to spoil ourselves, to relax and feel good emotionally and mentally is significant to help us be our best selves.

When we are married the need for self care becomes even more necessary, but in the marriage realm it can get highly problematic. Not only do you have to continue to provide that spoiling and special attention for yourself, you need to have the time and energy to also give it to someone else. Just because it's difficult to keep up with doesn't mean you can skip out on it. You wouldn't want their responsibilities of watching out for themselves to interfere with the responsibility they have with looking out for your needs, do you? If you're like me, you expect your guy to do both. Which means you have to do the same.

I realize that makes you wonder… "how is all this quality time supposed to happen? No one has the money, energy, let alone time to book endless spa appointments, or spoil themselves and each other senseless!" Aww sweetie, you aren't thinking deep enough. Sure pampering can be massages, pedicures, bubble baths, etc., but it's much more than that.

Pampering/spoiling yourself and someone else is simply about making one feel good inside and out. It's the romantic gestures big and small, it's how you react to and treat each other, it's the kind words, compliments and various ways you uplift and brace one another.

You can pamper each other's ego by making a big deal about something they have accomplished. Let me paint you a picture. Do you remember how excited you got when your kid was finally potty trained? You cheered them on and made them feel big and proud. If you don't have kids, I'm positive you still get the point. Stroking someone's ego is basically just like cheering on a kid because in a way, we are all just big kids. We like to feel special and receive attention. I know as a woman I love attention from my guy, but one thing I had to realize was the fact that my guy liked pampering and attention, too. Society would have us believe that praise and compliments are only something women long for, but that is simply not true.

Men also like to feel that they are potty trained pros. HA HA! The point is, no one likes to be overlooked all the time. Don't get it misconstrued, I am not saying my husband cries and whines all over the place, "love me Nicki, tell me how pretty I am." He's not that type at all. But, I discern a difference when I did unexpected things big and small to make him feel happy and appreciated. I noticed the sly little smile he would give when I said something nice about him in front of others or complimented him on how well he takes care of his family. Sometimes, the hard work, smart choices and remaining strong in the midst of tough situations demands a cheerleader and I was glad to be that for him.

Now that I think you understand, surely you are thinking of things you and he can do for each other. As usual, I will bet you are drawing a blank. Fine! I'll once again give you some ideas.

For us ladies, it's always a great idea to try our best to be the woman he married. Please don't go getting upset, use your head here. I'm not saying you still have to be that size 0, replace your vagina with the "before kids" version, and stay on top of everything like you were able to do at first. That shit is exhausting! Responsibilities increase as life goes on and it's hard to stay on top of everything.

I'm just saying, *try* (when you can) to do some of the things you did in the beginning. If you cooked for him at first, whip up a meal when time permits. Surprise him with lunch at the job, wear the sexy clothes, make sure you shave, no, wait, go get a wax instead. I finally got up the nerve to get one a few years ago and although it hurts like death torturing you on a hamster wheel, it is SO worth it!

Moving on, you could go to a sporting event with him, maintain your hair and makeup, be adventurous in and out of the bedroom, send him teasing texts, you get the gist. Do things he expects and things he doesn't. Keep him excited, on his toes and interested in what your next move may be. I know you are creative and you have tons of ideas when you really think about it. You just needed someone to get the ball rolling.

For men, it's about staying a gentleman: opening doors for you, holding your hand, rubbing your feet after a long day, complimenting you, listening when you need to talk, dealing with the kids, helping keep the house clean, surprising you with things for no reason, making dinner so you don't have to, carrying your shopping bags without complaint, giving you sex that's all about you, getting dressed up nice, keeping his hair cut, etc. There is so much they can do to keep you happy and feeling like the luckiest woman alive.

Yet sadly, I realize that men don't always do it. Cut him some slack, though. Sometimes as the marriage progresses, men generally forget. It doesn't mean he isn't attracted to you or that he no longer feels grateful for you, men are just slow with this. They may forget that you like small nice gestures, like roses when you come home or him giving you compliments. That's why it's important to make sure you are doing your part. Most people (husbands especially) learn from seeing. When you are kind to someone, in turn, it makes them want to be kind to you. Sure, this doesn't always happen, but most of the time it does.

Now, if you're continuously delivering "best wife ever" material and you look up to see that he hasn't even started executing his part for you, it's time to halt what you are doing and have a talk with him. If after the talk, he doesn't improve at all or makes changes and then goes back to the same "no appreciations given" lifestyle. Simply take a break from all that you do for him. Not to be mean, (well maybe just a little), but moreso to get him to recognize your worth. Only make meals for yourself (and the kids) and leave him none. Get dressed up nice for yourself, but don't let him touch or have any reward from all that sex appeal you are emitting. I told you, men are sometimes better with visuals. Experiencing the withdrawal of all the things you do makes it easier for him to notice how important you are, step up and give you your due diligence.

If you find that no matter what you do he STILL doesn't respond to you cutting off his VIP services, you need to find an intensely bold way to give him a dose of his own medicine. For example, let's say that every morning he goes to pee, he basically misses the toilet and gets most of it on the floor. You have repeatedly begged, pleaded and shouted for him to clean it up and not leave the repulsive, nauseating puddle on the floor for you to unknowingly step in. Nevertheless, he won't take action and the torturous routine you endure doesn't seem to phase him at all.

Well then, communicate in a way that he understands. Switch your translator from "Excuse Me Dear, Could You..." to "YOU BETTER LOOK THE FUCK OUT!" and press play. The next time your period comes on, leave a used, bloody pad, in the driver seat of his car. I'll bet he will NEVER forget the disgusted, angry and disrespected way he felt, for as long as he lives. I know, that's gross, but so is pissing on the floor and ignoring you when you asked him politely and repeatedly to stop, or at least clean up after himself. However, this is a hypothetical and any advice is merely a suggestion to get you thinking. I'm only trying to show you how to speak to those that don't understand words. It's ideal that if there is a problem you both should maturely fix the issue... without blood and urine of course. But hey, sometimes you just have to adjust your translator.

On the other hand, you may feel that leaving him, punishing him, getting on his level or talking to him isn't worth it. Although you wish he was kinder, more grateful, helpful and concerned with all that you do for him, he just isn't. You may feel that at least he pays the bills, and at the end of the day, you're willing to accept that. Well in my opinion your standards are pretty low, but I can still respect it. It is your life and your marriage and no one, and I do mean no one, can tell you when it's time to leave, stay, get down and dirty or speak up. That has to be completely your call.

However, let me suggest that if you do decide to leave, keep me on payroll. Deciding to say, "Sayonara!" to that sucker doesn't mean you need to let me go, too. I'm going to be the one to help you through dating and your next marriage. Just calm down and don't go making rash decisions. I'm just trying to state my case now because you might need to hear it if you are tossing people out of your life. Now, that we're clear on that, let's stop with the doom and gloom of relationships because I'm trying to make an uplifting point here.

You guys have to take care of each other. Be supportive of one another's dreams and off the wall ideas. Make one another feel smart, accomplished, cared for and attractive, as often as you can. Treating each other special helps you both gain confidence. As a result, you will perform better as individuals and as a unit.

I recall once when I wanted to start a business making candles. Even if my husband thought it was a dumb idea, he never said so. Instead, he asked me what could he do to help. We spent hours upon hours coming up with logo designs, company names, various scents I would sell, etc. He even went as far as to help me make the products, box them up and then deliver them. He was proud of me every time I got a sale and gave me motivation every time I didn't. Eventually, I lost interest because... well candles are just too much work! Yeah, I know ALL companies (especially new ones) take tons of work, but honestly I was getting bored. I just felt in my heart that my talents could be of better use elsewhere.

Point is, he never said a word. He just supported my decision to stop one business and start another, and another and then... you guessed it, another. He jumped into every venture with me with the same unconditional support and encouragement as he did with the first one. It's not like my "quick to abandon" companies were burning through thousands and thousands of dollars, so besides time wasted while I figured out things, there were no major losses.

Even still, I can only assume that being the bystander was not always a fun job for him, but it was what I needed so he obliged me. Spoiling me with his time, support, opinions and ideas to help me grow and I was thankful for it.

Then years later I finally figured it out. I wanted to be a counselor! But not some old, dry boring counselor that had to go to school for years just to get a degree. I wanted to be a modern day counselor. One that engaged their clients unlike any other. Drinking wine to make things casual and lighten the mood, using twisted metaphors and word play to improve people's lives and last but not least, calling them out on their shit and taking breaks when I deemed necessary. Yay me, right!

Obviously, that type of counselor didn't exist, so I had to create the job, then, fill the role. Talk about being busy, but I did it! I put aside my fears, excuses and wine glass, then headed to AA. Assholes Ambassadors University, of course, I call it AA for short. What else could AA stand for?

Anyway, I enrolled, went to school for a day (they have a fast turnaround) and then graduated. Sadly, I didn't graduate at the top of my class. That spot went to some politician, but I'm still proud. Now that I am self-certified and the CEO of my company, "Tipsy Counseling, LLC," no one can tell me anything.

Eventually, I told my husband of all my accomplishments and my new job that allowed me to be a counselor while drinking. As usual he was happy for me. However, I think I heard him mumble, "those poor bastards" under his breath. When I asked him to repeat it, he just smiled and said "nothing dear, you'll be great at it." You see, thanks to all that pampering my husband gave me, I was able to leave my comfort zone and come help you guys.

Sorry, I got slightly off subject there. I'm sure you don't care to know how I got where I am, you just want the information. So back to the pampering, spoiling, loving and supporting each other topic. It's a huge deal and obviously works, which means it shouldn't be overlooked.

Just don't forget that although I said take care of each other, I also mentioned not to neglect the love you owe numero uno. No one can take better care of you, than you yourself. Splurge every once in a while. Buy that purse that costs too much and the shoes to match. Every choice shouldn't be one or the other. Have that spa day, go see a movie with friends, sit in the quiet, make a vision board, go shopping, read a good book or whatever you need. Life will be there and you can jump back in the ring when you're ready to box. Do not let anyone make you feel guilty about taking care of yourself. You will be happy and so will he, which in turn gives your marriage the best version of you both. I guess, all I'm really trying to say is this... you may have many roles but those roles really only boil down to one job. That job is, to take care of one another, do me and yourself a favor and don't fuck this up!

Another random, just for you...
You know what? That concept I used where you vent your frustrations to things you can't change made me feel pretty good. I mean, it fixed nothing, traffic is still there, but I feel better that I let it all out. This wine I'm drinking tonight really has me ready to share more. Therefore, I think it's time to release my annoyance with my power meter and bill.

DEAR POWER BILL/METER,
Why are you so high? Every month I feel your numbers are different which is weird because my

place of residence doesn't get larger. What's with all the mood swings? Can we talk about this?

I feel you should only change twice a year. Once for summer and once for winter. I wish I knew how to read you, you're so mysterious. You have been attached to my home since forever and we never even speak. I normally forget you are there until I get a letter in the mail from you.

Maybe, it is my fault for not learning about you earlier in life, but in my defense, the other kids weren't doing it and I didn't want to seem uncool. Peer pressure and all, you know. I'm just asking you to consider making yourself more understandable so that we can become friends.

If your charges are lower next month, I will take that as a sign that you do have a heart and you are open to a friendship and bill lowering negotiations. Eagerly awaiting your response.

Signed,

Confused, happy, but somewhat sad, disappointed, a little itchy, glad I got paid, but not happy that you take so much of the money because you didn't work any of the hours, heated (but not too heated or else you may charge me more), so instead just the right temperature, trying to process my emotions, until next month.

T HE FINANCIAL FACTOR

When people say, "more money, more problems," are they in turn saying, "no money, no problems?" I don't think so. Which means, in a way, it's pointless to say that more money causes more problems. If in actuality money itself (regardless of the amount) can cause a multitude of problems, people that are broke and rich alike, argue that the other doesn't understand.

Although, I see valid points on both sides, I do find it funny that only those that are broke, want to trade places with those that are rich, and not the other way around. Why is this? If having money causes so many more problems, then why is it that I have never met a rich person that voluntarily wants to be broke? I think it's because no one really cares about the level of problems, they just want the money. Why wouldn't they? Money is fabulous and it makes life so much easier.

I'll bet it brings a smile to your face when you remember being single and having a pocket full of money. All the choices and limitations were on you. You could live where you wanted, buy what you wanted, eat what you wanted, wear what you wanted and not have to worry about checking with someone or hearing their opinions. It was YOUR money and you did with it, what you pleased. Then, you went off and got married and suddenly those money choices were no longer up to you, and that my friends, is when money can cause the most problems...

◆ ◆ ◆

I always tell my husband his money is my money, and my money is my money. It's just a joke that I say because typically, I'm the one who will spend up all his money (if he lets me) and all my money. Although, it gets a laugh out of both of us, I know money issues aren't always so lighthearted or easy. Your goals may not be their goals and your ways of handling money certainly may not be theirs. One person could be more of a saver while the other is labeled the spender. Using my marriage as an example, my husband is definitely the saver. I, on the other hand, like to shop and nice things seems to have my number on speed dial. They lure me out to buy them and more often than I'd like to admit, I usually cave. I think I have this need to feel rewarded. Like, if I work super hard I deserve that new shirt, purse, shoes or car. I mean life is stressful, right?!

Anyway, it's not always a good thing because saving is important. You have to think about your future. Retirement won't be such a fun, relaxing and carefree deal if you only have a tiny, constipated account balance. It's bad enough to struggle when you are younger, but the idea of struggling financially when you are older is scary. I have to remind myself of this when a hot new item calls my name. Surprisingly, envisioning an older version of myself begging for money has definitely helped. Sure, I can get some things, but I don't need everything and most importantly, I don't need everything right now.

The more I watched others to see if they had the same dilemmas I did, the easier it became to realize that every couple had uneven financial habits. Nonetheless, the goal is to find what works best and keep at it for as long as possible. Kind of like hitting that right position during sex in order to reach a powerful orgasm. In this case, the orgasm is an overflow of money that leaves you smiling every time you think about it. HA! That's an interesting thought, if orgasms equalled money, with all the clueless performances of some of these men out here, many women would be broke.

Anyhow, I like to keep things simple for you, so I have come up with five categories to roughly sum up the various ways couples handle their finances.

The first is "Money Sharers." These people, in their financial benevolence, combine ALL their dinero. Typically, they have a joint bank account where their income is deposited. If an unexpected bonus or monetary gift is received, they are likely to combine this as well because they feel all money should be merged in order to gain financial success. Once all dollars have been accounted for, they jointly decide how it will be spent.

Bills, miscellaneous activities, debt, travel, savings, etc. are all given a specific payout. If something is missing or doesn't add up accurately, it is highly likely that these types are able to refer to their meticulously balanced checkbooks to locate the probable cause. Month after month and day after day, they put their money (and brains) together to work out a plan that not only places them on the right financial path, but keeps them there. I actually look up to people in this category because they are more financially focused than I could ever be.

The second is "Money Some-Timers." I think my husband and I fall more under this category. These people tend to have a joint account for household spending and savings. However, they also have separate bank accounts to handle personal needs and wants. It is not expected or likely that they will pull every single dime together to determine where it will go. Although, they both have control over the joint account they tend to not have access to each other's personal account.

Their patterns involve looking over the household expenses, getting them paid, setting joint financial goals and then, they are basically on their own. They are no stranger to helping each other out financially or sharing money if the need arises, but they'd rather keep some level of their incoming dollars separate.

The third is "Money Separators." Now these people are the "Mr. and Mrs. Smith" of the financial world. Quick side bar, that was a good movie right? Brad and Angelina, living separate lives, at each others throats and tearing up that gorgeous house... I loved it!

At any rate, these married bankers keep money as separate as possible. In this scenario there is no joint bank account. Once they got married, they simply kept their own private account to deal with any monetary obligations. I wouldn't even be surprised if people in this category don't know exactly which bank their significant other uses. They treat their finances as if they are two companies. His and Hers. Their money never crosses over. They faithfully provide their agreed upon financial contributions on time and without fuss. If one does need to borrow money from the other, they always make sure to pay their spouse back. I could never do that, if he gives me money, it's lost forever. Ha ha not really... but seriously, yes, he'll never see that money again.

The fourth is "Money Sitters." This category applies when there is one major bread winner in the house. A common example is when the husband works and the wife is a stay at home mom. I refer to the bread winner as the "Sitter" or "Babysitter" of the money because they are responsible for making sure the financial needs of the household are met.

Let me point out that this situation does not mean that the unemployed spouse is lazy, can't handle the task of taking care of the household or doesn't earn their own income through various ventures and such. I'm simply saying any income they earn, is not depended upon, for the survival of the household. They may even be the one who collects the money from the working spouse and then determine how the bills will be paid. Therefore, bread winner or not, financial decisions are still a team effort to them.

Even still, with this approach to finances, both parties have to be careful. Sometimes people become arrogant in their position and feel that making all the money, equals making all the decisions, and that IS NOT TRUE! When you are married you support each other, because you love each other. Stay away from being obnoxious, disrespectful and making asshole moves that undermine the opinions and wishes of your other half. No one should be looked down upon because they aren't earning an income that is equivalent to the other. Besides, making money isn't the only way a person contributes to a marriage.

Continuing in that line of thought, what if you are the only employed spouse, but you haven't agreed on that? You have continually, calmly, kindly but firmly told them you need them to contribute to the finances because things are not going so well. Yet, no matter how much you have pleaded for their help, they'd rather be... dare I say it...lazy and ignore your patience and endless requests.

Well, I think it's time for you to go about this as a solo mission. Take it upon yourself to cut out the things that aren't necessary. Make the sole decision to save money and cut corners where it's needed. If they get angry that you didn't consult them, calmly remind them of all the times that you have tried to ask for their financial assistance and how they have done nothing.

Understand that I am NOT saying to mistreat or disregard them if they are actively trying to find work and just haven't been successful. But if they are genuinely ignoring you and all the financial burdens are on your shoulders, then cutting out their extra unnecessary activities as well as a few of your own, is a MUST no matter if their feelings get hurt or not. Unfortunately feelings, don't pay bills.

The last is "Money Shitters." You don't have to stretch the imagination too far, the name says it all. These people shit money away like it's nothing, which is why they are considered financially immature. They barely save a dime and continuously spend on frivolous things. Travel, restaurants, impulse purchases, new clothes, personal hobbies, endless video games, etc. are just a few of the splurges they choose over smarter financial decisions. It wouldn't be uncommon if these two didn't posses a bank account to put money in. Since it's normal behavior for them to spend their entire check within a short period of time, having a bank account would just be a waste of paper. A deeper look into their relationship can reveal that either one or both of them are the reason to blame for their finances being in the toilet.

Honestly, I think it may be less frustrating if both parties are irresponsible. Somehow one spouse trying to financially succeed while the other is content with failure seems worse. Could you imagine how infuriating it is to be married to someone like that? If you're spouse does fit the bill as the wasteful type, I feel for you. Here you are, desiring to do better, build up savings, buy a house, a car or an actual bed frame to put your mattress in, yet your other half spends their money on endless "in the moment" items.

Truth be told unless you want both of you to end up homeless and hungry then I suggest you step up and take charge. Yes, spouses that collectively correct their finances are ideal, but it doesn't always happen. So confront them, but be ready to go at it alone if you need to. Sinking with the boat is your only other option and I don't think you need to let their immaturity consume and then destroy your ability to do better.

So there it is, the break down of the five financial categories as I have seen them unfold. Do I have an opinion of which one works best? Nope.

Whether you are broke, rich or somewhere in between, as long as it's working for you guys then I certainly have no complaints.

However, you may have noticed that I always recommended that if you're the responsible spouse, it is your job to step up and do the financial handling/planning for both. Understand that I didn't say that because I don't think it would be a good idea to simply leave their ungrateful ass. It's because you obviously love them and aren't ready to leave. This issue may only frustrate you but that doesn't mean you see it as a deal breaker. Plus, as I have said before, I never tell people to leave their marriage. That is a decision that a couple needs to decide on their own. If things can't be worked out then you two will know before anyone else.

Keep in mind, financial challenges arise with everyone no matter what approach they choose. Don't freak out if there are bumps in your monetary road. Navigating what works best will be a frequent activity because rarely is any couple fully a Sharer, Some-timer, Separator, Sitter or Shitter. Most of us are a combination of two, three or all five, depending on what's going on in life.

Even though, I'm assuming you already know which category is more or less your position on finances, I'm still going to provide some questions for your consideration, to stay (or get) on track.

Do you share information pertaining to work income? Should you disclose all money that you receive? Gifts? Bonuses? Money you find on the street? Who makes the most money? Does that matter to either of you? Does it create financial friction? If so, why? Are the bills split evenly? One handles everything? Are both parties ok with this agreement? Do you think both of you are doing the best you can in regards to money? Do you have a budget? Do you wish to save more? Less? How should personal purchases be handled? Is it none of their business? Fully their business? Is a joint account needed? Can you both spend money out of the joint account? Or should only one person control that? Are separate accounts a good idea? Should your spouse have access to your personal account for emergency purposes? What about vice versa? What are your financial future goals? Is there a certain amount you want to have saved? Have you sat down to make sure that number will work? What are you doing to make your financial goals a reality?

Don't forget that money, is a yet another highly delicate, and in a way scary subject. It can easily cause complications and in some cases, drive people apart. Money mindsets between spouses are rarely running on the exact same track. Even the best couple can agree that they still have monetary hiccups every now and again. In order to avoid major catastrophes over it, be open and direct about financial decisions, expectations and limitations.

Don't allow the differences of money to destroy your household or turn you against one another. Money is meant to take care of you and your family, not divide it. Even if you are not earning enough to meet the goals you desire, no worries. Opportunities will arise that give you a chance to make the investments, purchases or vacations you feel you've missed. Luckily, there will always be millions of dollars in the world, but don't take for granted that there is only one him, and one you.

Well, it's time for me to call it quits for this evening. Don't be sad, I'll be back tomorrow to chat with you a bit more. It's Friday, so that means time for date night. Some nice restaurant with a fancy dish has my name on it. Last week's date night was laid back. We went to see a football game and got full from hotdogs, nachos, alcohol, etc. It was awesome! Oh, before I go, remember I told you about the girl who gave her guy head on the toilet? Well, a different friend said, with a few changes (like smell, position, etc) she would be curious to do it. She got a "we regret to inform you letter" to end our friendship immediately. Yuck!

Bringing the Session to a Close

As I sit here with my glass of wine in one hand and the TV remote in the other. I can't help but think... should I watch Bridesmaids or Resident Evil? I don't know if I'm in the mood for girly or gory. Either I must be close to my period or I need to pee on a stick because that's when I get annoyingly indecisive. All I know is, my husband better watch out and stay the hell away from my ice cream!

In case you are wondering, date night went well. I was irritated because it took the waiter forever to bring our food, but we ended up getting our entire meal for free so... worth it. I hope that you do special things with your guy and keep your vows victorious as well. Marriages aren't going to run themselves, you know! The goal isn't for you to just be husband and wife, it's for you to be best friends for life. Tell each other everything, be open, laugh together, keep God first, lock the kids or pets away when you need quiet time and be a spouse that your other half can be proud of. It's much easier to enjoy your marriage when you like each other.

Anyway, I can admit that I may have left out a whole lot of things. I aimed to cover every major subject that I felt could pose a threat to your marriage if underused or overlooked, but some of you have marriages that have been places mine hasn't. I am still figuring this marriage thing out and there are mountains I have conquered and others I have yet to climb. Even still, I am more than positive that at least some of my ramblings have given you very valuable insight.

Bearing my heart on my sleeve, I must admit that I really like you. Hopefully, my bluntness didn't scare you too bad. If it did, I think there is a training you can go to for thicker skin. Sure, sometimes I can be harsh, maybe even hurtful, but I mean it all in love. I want you to succeed, I want your marriage to succeed. I want us to stay tied to the ball and chain together. People on the outside don't get it (or maybe they do which is why they aren't married), but marriage is hard. In the same breath, it is also wonderful. Sometimes, you need the point of view from someone already in the box to help you see how much of a gift it is.

However, all jokes aside, I do have something very important to tell you. Put down your glass, silence your phone, give your kid that candy bar they keep asking for and turn on whatever sports game your guy is into so that you have no distractions. Are you ready? Good.

You do know, that it doesn't matter if you put into effect every tip I gave you, read all the books on marriage available and do every other thing you can think of, including bending over backwards, that your marriage IS NOT going to be perfect, right? We are all just human. Ups and downs, shortcomings and hurt are a part of the journey. Your husband may never become the great communicator that you want him to be, his sex moves may never be better than a 70's porn star and his way of dealing with money may never totally line up with yours, but that is all ok. In contradiction to his best attempts, his internal wiring could be faulty. The same truths goes for whatever your flaws are.

Sometimes, you are going to have to work harder in certain areas in the marriage that he will continuously fall short on and he will have to do the same for you. For example, carrying 60% (or more) of the load in household chores while he carries 40% (or less) isn't uncommon. Some guys are just not that neat. They don't always mean any harm or think that your efforts are worthless. It's just that their arms can only stretch far enough to put the dirty clothes next to the laundry basket, not actually inside of it. A real bummer, I know.

On the flip side, he may handle 80% of the mechanical and gross work in the house while you only handle 20%. For some reason you can't muster the courage to kill and then, pick up that scary, gigantic bug that tried to run you out of your house.

Do not let the uneven balance in some areas destroy the whole thing. Everything in a marriage does not always come out to 50/50. You are in this to help each other out where the other falls short. Yes, people can improve, but don't expect perfection. However, use your head, it's not your job to carry the majority or full load of EVERY, SINGLE AREA of your marriage. That's called being a step stool and it's not fair and needs to be addressed. I'm not worried, though. I have confidence that you are smart enough to know if you are dragging around a dead weight versus being a help mate to a good man.

In the unfortunate event that you did decide that marriage isn't for you or your spouse wants out, don't beat yourself up about it. Ironically, there is, sometimes, beauty in goodbye. You live and you learn, so apply the knowledge and keep it going. We are not perfect creatures, you must shed your tears, then pick up the pieces and reassemble. I'm sorry I don't have more advice for you, but my prayers are with you that you find your happiness in life.

OK, you can now pick back up your wine glass. Thanks for giving me your full attention for that crucial bit of information.

◆ ◆ ◆

Hey! I just heard the music for Friends on TV. This is the episode where Ross does something to Rachael and she doesn't like it. I want to see it, so my glass and I will be back in a bit to continue...

◆ ◆ ◆

I'm back. For you that was probably only about 5 seconds, but I left you guys for a couple of hours. That was such a good episode. The verdict is still out on whether or not I feel they were on a break though. Actually, I didn't even finish the whole episode because mid way through, I saw my husband in the hallway, he was looking good, one thing lead to another and then... well you guys don't want to hear about all that.

Anyway, I will be done with this marriage session completely in just a moment, because I think I have something else I'd rather be doing. If you need me, I can be found on Amazon or some platform like it, coaxing unknowing (and likely unwilling) people to attend my counseling sessions. You know what? This was fun! I had an awesome time providing positive encouragement and guidance to everyone. To be totally transparent, discussing these topics even helped me re-exam the structure, hopes and goals of my marriage all over again. If it did that for me, I am confident that it did the same for you.

Think about it, I helped you with your kids, your in-laws, communication skills, pampering each other, medical set backs, dealing with traffic, not being intimidated by other relationships, and even your sex life. Most counselors would just give you the constant, "How did they make you feel?" line and let you figure out your problems on your own. By using my own life lessons so that you can laugh at or with me and still learn, I feel I did more than that. Don't misunderstand me, it's not that I don't think traditional counseling works, it really does and those counselors are bad ass. They are out there everyday helping people that are on all levels of fucked up and still manage to stand, smile and stay sober. God bless them!

However, as effective as their methods are, my version of self-help is a necessary alternative. It's a divergent and unapologetic approach. For some, the experience of something different, is the exact dose they need to finally improve and be *someone* different.

So count yourself lucky, and when your husband is balls deep in you, wearing his favorite shirt and kissing up to your sweet ass for all those wonderful sex moves, you can just smile and thank me, because you know what.... you're welcome.

◆ ◆ ◆

Keep reading for a preview of the next book in the series!

The *not so* Tipsy Pregnancy Counselor

Coming 2019

UGH! What has his sperm done to me?!! Oh please, don't act like that is a gross thought, you're pregnant now, gross is about to become your roommate. Anyway, I feel like it's in war mode and attacking any and everything inside my body it comes into contact with. I'm speechless because I've been with my husband for years. Shouldn't his militant semen assassins know me by now?

When I saw that big fat positive we were so happy. We even went out and celebrated and I felt awesome. Now I've become a zombie that somehow still has the ability to feel cramps, nausea and emotions! Pregnancy is supposed to be beautiful, it's supposed to be freeing. The only thing I've freed is my breakfast, my dinner and my lunch from 2 days ago. I hope they can start delivering mail next to this toilet because I don't think I'm going anywhere any time soon.

You know what? Let me just take a deep breath and calm down. I wanted this and I'm glad to be expecting. Currently I'm just getting more expectations than I bargained for. I have no food left to get rid of and I don't think my body is going to accept dry heaving as sufficient much longer. I feel like death's favorite… OH SHIT, I have to go… here comes an organ.

ABOUT THE AUTHOR

Nicki Grace is a wife, mother and author from Atlanta, GA. You can follow her blog at thetipsycounselor.com

42731016R00074

Made in the USA
Columbia, SC
17 December 2018